The New Careers

The New Careers

Individual Action and Economic Change

Michael B. Arthur,
Kerr Inkson and
Judith K. Pringle

SAGE Publications
London • Thousand Oaks • New Delhi

First published 1999

Reprinted 2003

SAGE Publications Ltd
6 Bonhill Street
London EC2A 4PU

SAGE Publications Inc.
2455 Teller Road
Thousand Oaks, California 91320

SAGE Publications India Pvt Ltd
32, M-Block Market
Greater Kailash – I
New Delhi 110 048

British Library Cataloguing in Publication data

A catalogue record for this book is available from the British Library

ISBN 0 7619 5931 9
ISBN 0 7619 5932 7 (pbk)

Library of Congress catalog card number available

Typeset by Mayhew Typesetting, Rhayader, Powys
Printed in Great Britain by Biddles Ltd.,
Guildford and King's Lynn

Contents

Author notes

Michael Arthur is Professor of Management at the Sawyer School of Management, Suffolk University, Boston. He is an editor of both "The Boundaryless Career" (Oxford University Press, 1996) and the "Handbook of Career Theory" (Cambridge University Press, 1989), and an author of numerous popular and scholarly articles on career-related topics. Michael has also been a Visiting Professor at the University of Warwick, UK, the University of Auckland, New Zealand, and London Business School. He holds his PhD from Cranfield University, UK.

Kerr Inkson is Professor of Management Studies at The University of Auckland, New Zealand. Kerr trained as a psychologist and was a member of the well-known "Aston Group" of organization researchers at the University of Aston, UK, before emigrating to New Zealand. He is author or co-author of many journal articles and six books, including academic works, textbooks and 'popular' books. He was first author of "Theory K" (1986) the most popular management book in New Zealand's history. Kerr holds a PhD from the University of Otago, New Zealand.

Judith Pringle is a senior lecturer in Department of Management and Employment Relations at the University of Auckland. She earned her PhD in psychology from the University of Otago before engaging in consulting and academic work in Australia and New Zealand. Her interest in reframing careers comes from a special interest in women's experiences. Her publications and research interests are in: feminist critiques of management and organizational theory, women-run enterprises across different ethnic groups, and transcultural research.

Preface

The origins of this book trace back to late 1993, when Michael Arthur and Kerr Inkson first met, and when the concept of "the boundary-less career" was first being voiced. Within two years, Michael Arthur was on sabbatical leave in Auckland and collaborating with both Kerr Inkson and Judith Pringle on the research reported in this book.

At the outset, our intention was a vague one: to gather data about what we perceived to be new career realities and to relate that data to new theories about careers that were coming into view. As we sharpened our focus, we found that Karl Weick's work on the *enact-ment* of careers emerged as a particularly helpful framework. Our respect for that framework is evident throughout this book.

In embarking on our work, we did not want to be constrained by any limited social or occupational group, or locus of employment, or further institutional interests in the course of careers. We did want to hear the voices of working people themselves, individuals from different socio-economic backgrounds, with different work histories and employment experiences. We also wanted to collect data that were illustrative of the uncertainties and hardships in career patterns that were being reported globally.

We chose a research setting and an approach to highlight global phenomena. Our data were collected in New Zealand, a country which, as we show in Chapter 2, is representative in population make-up, economic development, and political fashion of the western block of the Organization for Economic Cooperation and Development (OECD) of which it is a member. The data reported are, there-fore, representative of the career context of developed economies, and directly relevant to an international audience.

In the last 20 years, many countries have made a major shift from relatively static, socialized economies to the more dynamic, enterprise-oriented economies favored as this book goes to press. Remarkably, such shifts have gained support from the center, even from the center-left, in many countries. In New Zealand, the shift was sudden, and once taken was encouraged by both major political parties over the ten-year period we investigate. Our data may therefore offer an especially sharp illustration of the global transformation toward the "New Economy."

As we elaborate in Chapter 1, the New Economy is characterized by dynamic, competitive, and technology-driven global forces in which the creation and flow of knowledge is a key consideration. This characterization stands in contrast to the "Industrial State" of large, and largely stable, corporations and public sector institutions presumed after World War II, and upon which most work in the careers field has been built. A principal purpose behind our work was to gauge people's readiness for, and adaptability to, the New Economy.

We owe particular thanks to a number of people, including Karl Weick for his inspiration, Denise Rousseau for helping lay the groundwork, and Karen O'Shea for her work as research assistant in arranging and conducting interviews with some of our early participants. We are also grateful to a cluster of colleagues who have believed in and encouraged us along the way, including but not limited to Loic Cadin, John Deeks, Robert DeFillippi, Regina O'Neill, Polly Parker, Michael Powell, Boas Shamir, and John Van Maanen. Thank you, also, to the many others who have been kind enough to listen as our research journey unfolded, and to give the benefit of their advice.

Both Suffolk University and The University of Auckland gave generous support to this venture. We would also like to acknowledge Jawad Hussein and Dessi Kjosova for particular help with computer-based case analysis, and our families for supporting us as we pursued our task. We are also deeply grateful to the 75 research participants who so generously gave their time and their candor in supporting our work. Most of all, this book is for them, and the everyday working persons whom they represent.

Michael B. Arthur
Kerr Inkson
Judith K. Pringle

1 Careers, Employment, and Economies in Transition

Spinning into New Opportunities

Peter left school at 17, followed his father into computing, and settled into a pattern of on-the-job learning. Several years and several companies later, he had risen to be data processing manager of a travel firm, where he "redeveloped their entire system . . . and sort of outgrew it." Peter then approached the travel firm's computer supplier, a major multinational company which we will call Infotex, and asked to work for them.

He started at Infotex as a branch support manager, where for the first time he supervised people who, he realized, had higher competency than he had. In a team environment with no obvious hierarchy, he learned political skills in order to protect his people from external pressures. He also gained some exposure to selling, and eventually asked the company for a direct sales opportunity as an account representative, in order to acquire new skills associated with the sales process. He was relocated to look after the company's largest national account, where his technical skills were valued. Having learned what he could about selling, including its unwanted pressures, Peter asked for another transfer.

This time he moved into a project management role at his original location, which provided broader experience in client systems; he was also a mentor to project team members. Soon he added a travel company to his client portfolio, leveraging his earlier experience in, and knowledge of, the travel industry. The combination of his expertise and his company's products enabled him to head a major sales initiative Infotex would not otherwise have pursued. He worked directly with the local chief executive officer, and gained an exposure to strategic sales. With Peter central to the company's sales effort, it successfully landed a large account. Corporate life, according to Peter, was "a hell of a lot of fun . . . there was champagne to be had." He was highly regarded by his CEO, and clearly on a fast track up the Infotex career ladder. He presumed he'd be there a long time.

But there were storm clouds on the horizon. The multinational parent company had over-extended itself, and it embarked on a phase of rapid downsizing. Peter was asked to be local support manager through this period, downsizing the company operations in which he had been so successful, and laying off his own colleagues. He was told: "Don't expect to have employment in Infotex in six months." But he wanted to see the work through because of the experience he would gain, and his feelings for the people involved.

A reduction in staffing was required, to which the still-profitable national company had to respond. Peter's boss came up with a creative solution. He asked Peter and some of his colleagues to start a "spinoff" venture, based on Infotex clients and the software that Peter and others had developed. Clients could receive ongoing support, and Peter and his colleagues could make a fresh start. Peter was the lead member of a group of three partners in the venture, along with nine other employees from the multinational's former staff.

The spin-off company has now been trading for several years. Peter's first marriage broke up, but he re-married one of the original employees of the new company. Their joint work in the company is central in their lives. The venture has been successful, both in finding new business on its own, and as a software venture partner to the slimmed-down Infotex. It now has 40 employees, and continues to grow. As managing director, Peter focuses his attention on a strategic vision of making his company world-class in software development. At 38, he looks forward, in the next few years, to moving on to new career investments.

Peter's story begins in the way we have been accustomed to think about work and careers: getting started in a chosen occupation or industry, finding a good company, contributing to the company, and being rewarded with steadily increasing status and salary. What changed Peter's career course was a reversal in his company's fortunes. Like many large companies, Infotex found it impossible to keep the implicit promises it had made to Peter and others. In the end, some of the investments that Peter and others had made in the company were returned to them. They were left to fend for themselves, and to make of it what they could. Peter's challenge was to apply his emergent occupational, industrial, managerial, and entrepreneurial talents in new employment circumstances. He was in the vortex of change, moving from an apparently secure position as a versatile corporate servant in a familiar company culture to a leadership role in a fledgling operation whose culture he and his colleagues had to create.

Peter was fortunate that his pace of learning, driven largely by his own initiative, was equal to the challenge. In exercising his initiative, he made sure that each job in his old "organizational" career helped to prepare him for new challenges, whatever they might be. He was also fortunate that much of his network from Infotex – colleagues, ex-colleagues, customers, and what was left of Infotex itself – remained intact, and provided the basis for his later success. Peter's expertise and his relationships, developed in his old company, became more important to him than the company itself.

Peter's story is in many ways typical of the careers we found during our research. Not everyone changes companies and becomes a CEO, but most people change companies with relative frequency. Not everyone moves on with such clear advantages – in personal abilities, networks, and business opportunities – as Peter held, but most have to work out, as he did, how to evaluate and mobilize accumulated learning and relationships in novel situations. Peter's story also touches on other themes that affect us all: the choice of occupation and its openness to new initiatives, the level of invest-ment in formal education versus on-the-job experience, the family context in which career decisions are made, the breadth of support systems and their usefulness in assisting adaptive career behavior, the level of acceptance of, or resistance to, company-prescribed career arrangements, and the challenge to integrate career and broader life activities.

Traditional Approaches to Careers

In exploring the dynamics of Peter's career, and the other careers reported in this book, we turn first to traditional career theory, theory that has long recognized the connection between careers and personal fulfillment. Underlying this recognition is the commonly accepted academic definition of "career" as "the evolving sequence of a person's work experiences over time."[1] If we acknowledge that, for many, "work" takes up perhaps 50 hours a week and "time" at work unfolds for 40 or 50 years, the significance of the career experience becomes apparent. Also, in marked contrast to other approaches to the study of work and employment, career theory emphasizes the time perspective through which unfolding experiences come about. Much as we might learn from a time-bound study of Peter's work as computer programmer, sales manager, or managing director, a career perspective asserts that we can only truly understand each step by reference to the "evolving sequence" of steps which have preceded and influenced it.

However, much early work on careers was driven by practical, interventionist considerations. During World War II, for example, the armed forces tackled major shortages and wastage of manpower by means of rigorous personnel selection and vocational place-ment based on "scientific" techniques of individual assessment and aptitude testing.[2] In the post-war boom, large companies sought to build stable, expert, and long-term workforces by developing intra-company "manpower planning" and "career planning" systems and incentives for valued staff to demonstrate career-long loyalty.[3] Career studies reflect the pragmatic biases of the technicians of employment. The vocational counseling industry is interested in careers as opportunities for individual choice and job-matching which extend the armed forces approach. The profession of "human resource management" seeks to enable companies to achieve business goals through the cultivation of stable workforces.

The vocational counseling approach adopted "trait-factor" theories based on human typologies which assume that work-related human characteristics are stable over a lifetime. These characteristics could then be matched to appropriate career (commonly called "vocational") choices and progressions.[4] A prominent outcome was the emergence of psychological testing in career advising and employee selection, premised on getting "the right person for the job." A variant on trait-factor theory brought early work experience into the picture, but still asserted that people put down "career anchors" for most of their working lives.[5] The fledgling practice of human resource management emphasized a different kind of stability, stemming from Weber's classical notion of "bureaucracy," of which the hierarchical "career system" was a key component.[6] The bureaucratic framework provided a way to assign responsibilities consistent with people's abilities, and to promote the careers of "fast-track" or "high potential" employees through successive job experiences.

Both the vocational guidance and human resource management approaches made uneasy accommodations with emerging ideas about "human potential." One accommodation was to promote the notion of "good jobs" combining employment stability with a respect for skills and work experience. Another was to encourage people to pursue their potential through a planned, career-long, and hierarchical ascent in a paternalistic firm.[7] However, in these accommodations the career actor was still viewed as a relatively inert resource whose development could be rationally influenced in the best interests of the company. The view prevailed that a career was "a succession of related jobs arranged in a hierarchy of prestige, through which persons move in an ordered (more or less predictable) sequence."[8] The human potential movement's claims about individual uniqueness, and feminist and minority claims about discrimination, were downplayed. So, too, were arguments that considerable life and work experience was a necessary precondition to people finding and realizing their own career potential.[9]

A different approach was taken by developmental theorists, who sought to find age- or stage-related patterns of career development. In the context of the individual's wider social roles as a family member, spouse, parent, etc., periods of exploration, consolidation, and change – such as the well-known "mid-life crisis" – can be plotted against age and family stage.[10] Developmental theories attempt to deal with the career as something more than a series of adjustments to the right job, or a pattern of chess moves imposed on a human pawn by a clever corporate employer. Rather, a career is seen as a dynamic developing entity, cumulative and recursive. It is true that precise correlations of age, stage, and career behavior are difficult to demonstrate, and that phases tend to be repeated.[11] However, the greatest value of development theories is not in the detail of the patterns they seek to discern in a shifting economic world, but in their focus on careers as organic entities, with developing life-cycles, which are shaped by complex interactions between personal make-up and choice, and the external forces of family, class, and economic and organizational circumstance.

What Traditional Lenses Show

How does traditional career theory help us to come to terms with the events of people's lives? Does it, for example, help us to understand Peter's career? Trait-factor theory enables us to recognize and even measure his "computer programming aptitudes" or "sociability" or "entrepreneurial career anchor"[12] and to relate these to his career progress. Human resource management theory might provide some basis for Infotex to ensure that Peter's talents were well used as his career developed. However, Peter apparently succeeded by coming to terms with his own attributes through "trial-and-error" career experimentation. He succeeded because he did not have a stereotyped view of his own capabilities, but instead had a generalized urge to explore and develop them. He progressed at Infotex even though apparently neither he nor the company had a conscious plan for his career. His choices were largely driven not by careful human resource planning but by his own restlessness and opportunism in seeking change.

As for developmental theories, while we can certainly see discrete stages in Peter's career, we can also see stages in each job and project he undertook within it. One developmental approach suggests that a broad pattern for professional careers is one of successive phases of identity formation, competency development, relationship building, and leadership.[13] Peter's story confounds these patterns. As a compulsive learner in a rapidly changing industry, he is constantly formulating and reformulating his workplace identity. In each successive contrasting job, he seeks to develop new competencies. The building of relationships, both inside and outside employing companies, has been a vital part of his career since it began. Finally, as a "fast-track" company star Peter gained managerial responsibility early; he has been a leader in both his multinational and his spinoff company ever since. Like many of the careers we report here, his seems to tumble around integrated phases – albeit in an ascending, or spiralling, pattern – rather than progressing through discrete stages.

Rosabeth Kanter comes closer to the mark in distinguishing three types of career logics:[14] the professional, based on developing specialist occupational skills; the bureaucratic, based on advancement within a corporation; and the entrepreneurial, based on adding value through enterprise. But again, Peter's career appears to be (as Kanter allows) not a single type but a succession of phases representing the three types: the developing computer professional, the rising star in the local Infotex bureaucracy, and finally the entrepreneur, adding value simultaneously to his company, his reputation, and his bank balance. Closer inspection of the dynamics of his moves and his motives suggests, however, that Peter has always taken an entrepreneurial approach to his career development. Through his habit of learning new skills, he has consistently added value – knowledge as well as financial – to both himself and the companies for which he has worked. This conceptualization of entrepreneurial self-development in both employed and self-employed situations appears to be helpful as a means of understanding at least some non-traditional careers.

What Traditional Lenses Don't Show

Two things are missing from any traditional account of Peter's career. First, there lacks a sense of the unfolding subjective meaning of life and work to Peter himself as he made his various transitions and cycled through his different jobs. Second, there lacks a sense of the dynamic interplay between episodes of the career itself – as shown, for example, in Peter's accumulating and transformational learning, and his use of past contacts to build present business – and, even more so, between the career and the environment of economic institutions within which it is played out.

Consider the subjective meanings which Peter attributes to his work and job choices. At least twice in his career so far, he has taken on moves that didn't make "objective" sense. That is, they didn't represent immediate attainment of more money or of higher position or status. Indeed, relatively few careers travel uninterruptedly along established lines of occupational or organizational seniority. Peter's selective moves were made because of his internal, subjective, even emotional, assessment of what he wanted to do. Yet it is the objective side of the career – publicly observable, and marked by such symbols as occupation, qualifications, job title, status, salary, position in the structure, and c.v. details – that has gained most attention. This publicly understood aspect of the career, of course, gives a shared platform of comparison, and allows for collective interpretation of people's career situations. However, the objective side of careers prevails to the neglect of the more personal, subjective side.[15] A principal aim of this book is to correct the balance.

A second aim, however, is to go beyond subjective experience. We also seek to show how – improbably, in relation to our conventional models of business causality – careers play their own special part in framing the economic forces which so often are assumed to be framing them. Peter's career and his economic environment are mediated by his subjective sense of his unfolding development in a changing world. His story comes to life for us because we see how his successive choices and experiences fit together and gather cumulative meaning. Peter's subjective career behavior is projected onto his surrounding environment, and onto the companies and causes he serves. The environment responds, notably when his boss rewards his loyalty and enterprise by putting a major business opportunity his way. Thus, career behavior becomes a two-way street. The outcome is that, although Peter is no longer a member of his old company, he still carries the legacy of the company with him, in experience, in opportunity, and in the support of others. In this sense, as we live out our careers, we are all like Peter. We are both products and producers of the work environments in which we participate.

Peter's odyssey is a personal journey, which involves personal decisions and builds personal fulfillment. But it is much more. As he travels, his decisions and his development change the world around him. His computer skills and the self-confidence which he developed in his early career changed Infotex. His energy provided Infotex with new software and new clients. As he migrated restlessly around the company, he transported, and blended into its substance, the competencies which were his stock-in-trade. He helped to shape Infotex strategy and its success. When Infotex downsized, the fragments of his experience – some within him, others now part of the company's texture – were shaken like the bits of colored glass in a kaleidoscope, a new pattern for a new situation.

Peter's boss could see a yet wider pattern, involving not just Peter and others, but Infotex assets and obligations. Together, Peter and his boss acted on the new opportunities that they saw. And so, in Peter's new venture, as he continues to build his career, he also builds his company, and with it the economy. In pursuit of his personal goals, he accumulates and renews learning, focuses and refocuses his company's role and strategy in a changing world. He builds changing networks of business relationships (inside and outside the company), through which he will continue to develop both company and career. Career and enterprise become fused in a dynamic pattern of effect, reciprocation, and economic outcome.

From Industrial State to New Economy

To more fully understand today's employment circumstances, and the career thinking associated with them, we need to go back to the nineteenth century. The transformation from an agricultural to an industrial society brought in the factory, with its permanent, centrally defined, and tightly controlled work arrangements. Similar patterns of centralized work arrangements in government, the military, and the church gave rise to relatively stable bureaucracies in which expertise tended to be company-specific, and was hoarded in permanent jobs and hierarchical sequences of jobs which were seen as firmly under the employer's control. In a parallel development, the efficient specialization of work functions in the bureaucracy encouraged individuals to accumulate finely-tuned but narrow skills, and to progress in their careers along narrow paths prescribed by professional and trade institutions.

Later initiatives, responding to the depression of the 1930s and the aftermath of World War II, sought to reinforce this image of employment and career stability, and built a system of formal or tacit employment rights predicated on a largely unchanging world. The idealized company was a large, stable, hierarchical pyramid, and the idealized employee was a loyal, conformist, upwardly-mobile "organization man."[16] The era of the "Industrial State" was characterized by economist John Kenneth Galbraith as one where "the most conspicuous manifestation" was the so-called "modern large corporation" and where the rest of the economy was "diminishing in extent and . . . most nearly static." Galbraith celebrated the large corporation's advantage in forward planning, and saw such planning as the hallmark of the industrial era.[17]

In the wisdom of the day, we saw the world through Industrial State glasses. We presumed an orderly growth in national economies, in protected, enduring public sector institutions, in the wealth and employment of major corporations, and in the privileges and entitlements of the working population. This worldwide pattern of expectations underpinned a broad consensus about how the world of corporate employment should service long-term individual needs. We saw an "organizational society,"[18] – and within it "organizational careers" serving the great institutions which appeared to be the engines of prosperity – in an orderly pattern of gradual evolution. The career theory we developed made sense of what we saw. Corporate planning was to be the beneficiary as well as the sponsor of career planning.

We persisted, despite what with hindsight look like clear omens of change. In the emerging success of the large Japanese corporations, and the attendant claims to loyalty-based, lifelong employment systems, we saw the shimmering mirage of a perfect symbiosis between individual and company.[19] We celebrated large manufacturing firms even as many of those firms were beginning to decline.[20] But the omens were there. More and more, the key to competitive success became innovation. Bureaucracies proved stubbornly unable to innovate,[21] and companies in heavy engineering, car manufacture, and electronics went out of business, leaving their career specialists and company pyramid climbers stranded. As trade barriers fell and reforming governments deregulated their economies, fast-moving competitors with more flexible structures and employment systems outmaneuvered the established order.

The omens of change heralded what has been called a "New Economy" based on fundamentally different principles.[22] Planning, at least in the Industrial State sense, has had its weaknesses revealed. The carefully planned production line has become a barrier to flexible specialization. Planned, supposedly cost-saving, arrangements with suppliers have become impediments to suppliers' product understanding and to innovation. Carefully honed "vertical integration" of related production phases has become a constraint on dynamic market alignment.[23] "Managerial capitalism," whereby managers decided how to re-invest their companies' profits, has given ground to "investor capitalism," whereby investors insist on collecting the profits and making the decisions themselves.[24] If the byword of the Industrial State era was "planning," its equivalent in the new era is "flexibility." It is a word that turns conventional career thinking on its head.

Changing the Focus on Careers

The old ways of thinking still pervade our employment systems and the legal systems that support them. They also pervade the way we think and talk about work and careers. For example, popular use of the term "the organization" as a large bureaucratic employer began about 50 years ago, and reflects parallel popular connotations for "the organizational society."[25,26] Careers, whether in the private or public sectors, were expected to trace the hierarchical rigidities that society was held to maintain. That legacy is under attack from the New Economy, and the new employment policies that it demands. It is also under attack – as we will see – from the behaviors of career actors themselves.

How much has the study of careers changed to accommodate the transition to the New Economy? One perspective common to the majority of management-oriented research on careers and employment, presumes that little has changed in the world of work. The essence of such reports is that the world may be presumed to stay the same while finer evidence for established concepts and ideas is accumulated. In a recent review of five interdisciplinary journals, 75 percent of the research articles on careers addressed traditional intra-company rather than inter-company movement.[27] There was a disproportionate emphasis on large firms, rather than on the small-to-medium firms which provide most employment and new job growth. Sixty-six percent of a larger set of articles on employment presumed a static rather than a dynamic host environment. The review also showed that most studies of careers have continued to imply that it is the careers of managers and professionals, and their traditional hierarchical advancement in large corporations, which are the most worthy of attention.

Against this, there have long existed other traditions which take wider perspectives. Notably, the Chicago School of Sociology, active since the 1930s, used the concept "career" as a device to explore both individual identity and the formation of social institutions.[28] The School's study of careers embraced non-work as well as work experiences, and subjective as well as objective components. All adult members of society were credited with the potential to have a career, and in fact the study of careers frequently turned on relatively exotic and idiosyncratic groups such as taxi-dancers.[29] As we broaden our focus from professionals and managers in bureaucratic structures to all adults in more flexible and dynamic situations, and from the simpler confines of the employee role to the wider spaces of individual social and family roles, we move more and more toward the perspective favored by the Chicago School.

Further support for changing the focus on careers comes from psychologically-grounded ideas about people as "sculptors" of their own careers, and as the creators of personal meaning in their lives.[30] Broader support comes from the multiple social science perspectives beginning to draw on what has been called "new science."[31] These perspectives consistently emphasize the interdependence of a system's elements (in our case, careers) over time, rather than traditional one-way cause-effect relationships. The same perspectives also emphasize the elements' self-organizing properties in adapting to their surrounding environments.[32]

Engaging with Boundaryless Careers

One platform for exploring the consequences of increased employment mobility, and providing a counterpoint to traditional career theory, involves a focus on "boundaryless careers."[33] The boundaryless career perspective is also offered as a career-oriented response to the observable societal shift from Industrial State to New Economy. The perspective is based on the straightforward observation that because of the mobility documented above, nearly all careers cross multiple employer boundaries. Boundaryless careers are therefore prototypical rather than atypical.

Various consequences follow. Career actors draw validation from multiple employment situations, sustain wide inter-company networks, and develop multi-employer arenas of choice for the implementation of their careers.[34] The boundaryless career gives us a different yardstick for staying with the same employer, namely because of successive accommodations to personal learning and lifestyle agendas rather than because of simple loyalty. This yardstick also helps us rethink careers in relation to the dissolution of other traditional boundaries – notably, corporate boundaries of hierarchy and status, occupational, trade, and job boundaries of specialist skill and function, and social role boundaries separating work considerations from those of family and home.[35] The boundaryless career appears as a key mechanism in the functioning of project-based organizing in such industries as semi-conductors[36] and film-making,[37] in broader prototypes for twenty-first century careers to match twenty-first century organizations,[38] and in "intelligent career"[39] arrangements – based on new, more flexible employment principles – to interact with emergent "intelligent enterprise."[40]

It is important, however, not to become too carried away by the more spectacular, futuristic scenarios of a boundaryless career world, and the boundaryless successes of people such as Peter. We should not forget the economically disadvantaged, and those marginalized in insecure, low-skill jobs. Nor should we forget the "casualties" that the new employment era brings in its wake.[41] We should not allow the new rhetoric of "portfolio careers,"[42] "intelligent careers," "post-corporate careers,"[43] and "entrepreneurial careers"[44] to cause us to lose sight of the less fortunate. Peter's golden opportunity may have been the atypical counterpoint to a norm of boundaryless marginalization and alienation of the co-workers who were forced out of Infotex at the same time.[45]

However, what the "boundaryless career" does offer is the promise of fresh solutions. These include solutions where people stay in their companies not because of length of service but because of the market value of their skills; where new job aspirants are not discouraged by layers of privileges negotiated by job incumbents; where status and rank do not automatically disqualify people from applying their skills; where learning becomes a central rather than a peripheral condition behind employment arrangements; where past mobility may be seen as a symptom of a drive to learn rather than a propensity toward disloyalty;[46] and where career anchors external to any one corporation are encouraged.

We conclude that there is a need for a new kind of inquiry into careers to show what traditional lenses on careers have failed to show. Such an inquiry will help us to focus on how careers function in the New Economy; to re-assert the neglected subjective side of the career; to connect with recent ideas about boundaryless careers; to take us beyond artificial considerations with regard to corporation, occupation, and status, and to represent the breadth of the working population.

An Enactment Perspective on Careers

As we have said, Peter is unusual in his talents, his energy, and his good fortune. These assets enable us to write an account of a relatively spectacular and influential career. Other workers live quieter lives, and change things less. Yet, as we will show, all workers accumulate learning and develop networks, as Peter did. All workers use their accumulated resources to *enact* their careers upon the surrounding environment. As Karl Weick puts it, people act, "and in so doing they create the materials that become the constraints and opportunities they face."[47] As individuals enact their careers they enact the environment itself. The detail of Peter's career is unusual, but the essence is prototypical.

The enactment perspective stands in contrast to traditional career theories, which perhaps served developed societies well from the 1950s to the 1980s. Those theories, however, fall short of an adequate account of Peter's career in the late 1980s and 1990s. They were developed for a world that exists less and less: a world of stable occupational categories, of clear job definitions and progressions, of hierarchical organizational structures populated by status-seeking men, of rationality and career planning imposing order on a stable world. As the years have gone by, internal and external company boundaries have fallen away, swept aside by larger forces such as information technology, the globalization of business, the pressure of competition, and the development of flatter and more flexible forms of organizing.[48] The workforce has changed, too, not least by its feminization, as more and more women (typically with career patterns involving periods out of the paid workforce and with different and more flexible career aspirations than those of men) have moved into paid employment.[49] These changes demand an extension of career theory, as those involved in career intervention are beginning to recognize.[50]

In an earlier age, Peter might have remained a career information technologist, or a company servant of Infotex. The booming 1980s, the restructuring 1990s, and the helter-skelter growth of his industry created vast new unexpected opportunities to which a person of Peter's energy was bound to respond. Again, Peter is prototypical. An occupationally specialized world develops, and is developed by, occupational careers. A corporate world develops, and is developed by, corporate careers. What kind of careers does the new deregulated, globalized, information-age, economy develop? And, equally important, what kind of economy do the new careers develop?

"Strong" versus "Weak" Situations

The environment of careers is increasingly diffuse. One way to understand the change is in terms of the existence of "strong" and "weak" situations as environments for career development.[51] Strong situations are characterized by clear structures and salient guides to behavior; the scope for individual variation in response is minimal. Large bureaucracies, companies, and institutions with strong cultures are examples. The classic large military organization, with its strong external boundaries, powerful socialization systems, and tight, rule-bound hierarchy, epitomizes a strong situation. In weak situations, there is less prescription of individual behavior and people are better able to choose among alternative actions.

Weick notes that employment situations may not always be weak, but that "they are weakening."[52] External and internal boundaries dissolve, lower-level employees are empowered, job descriptions and status hierarchies are replaced by informally mediated opportunities to contribute. The new feminized workforce erases the barrier between work and home and finds ways to integrate previously separate social roles into new configurations. The tightly knit bureaucracies of the Industrial State era, or of the old, militaristic Japanese *zaibitsu*[53] are examples of strong situations. The loosely knit, project-driven, constantly metamorphosing industrial environment of Silicon Valley[54] is an example of a weak situation. Weak situations provide new opportunities for enactment, reduce the time span of reciprocal exchanges, and allow learning to be driven by individual rather than organizational agendas.

Much career behavior takes the form of companies attempting to impose strong situations on their employees, and their employees attempting to make them weak in order to provide a choice of career-relevant options. This is the source of Peter's resourceful enactment in corporate settings. Since companies are finding it more necessary to dismantle strong situations (to provide flexibility) and career actors increasingly seek to escape strong situations (to enhance career choice), future companies will more and more become arenas in which individuals are invited to find and make career-enhancing choices within the broad spectrum of the company's commercial activity. We are reminded of the story of a new employee of W.L. Gore and Co. who, on his first day, asked what his job was. The manager's answer: "Why don't you look around and find something you'd like to do?"[55] In such a system, control through job definition is replaced by encouraging energy through personal commitment. The situation is deliberately weakened, and people search for their own career choices in an open arena.

Reciprocities

Another key concept is that of *reciprocities*.[56] Reciprocities are the ties that bind career actors and their employers to one another. With each job experience, we engage in exchange: with the employer company, with managers and co-workers, and with the larger projects to which jobs frequently contribute. We give and we receive. In the simplest kind of employment contract, the individual gives labor to the employer and receives wages in return. Job descriptions, performance targets, formal contracts, and labor laws specify in detail the contribution the individual is expected to give to the employer and the extrinsic rewards he or she is supposed to receive in return. However, there is also a psychological contract[57] implicitly agreed upon between employer and employee, covering the less tangible expectations of both parties: for example, the employer's expectation of loyalty, or of "performance above and beyond the call of duty", the employee's expectation of fair pay, interesting work, autonomy, and fulfillment. To honor the contract, each side must engage in reciprocities toward the other.

Employer–employee reciprocities are prominent in Peter's story. Peter's thirst for new experiences led to his becoming more and more valuable to his old employer. The quality of the relationship developed over time and led to Peter taking on the management of a crisis situation when his company really needed it. If we may further anticipate the case study career data whose collection we describe in Chapter 2, consider the further example of Susan:

Playing Fair While Shopping Around

Susan had been encouraged in school to do science and proceeded to train and graduate as a food technologist. Despite some emergent misgivings abut her chosen occupation, she went to work for a meat company, and reports that she "saved them hundreds of thousands of dollars just by changing one ingredient" in a recipe, as well as developing new products and improving existing ones. In return, Susan gained experience in putting her theoretical skills into practice, and in the workings of a small business. In her next company, she found food technology work repetitive, but was able to draw on her business exposure to transfer to a marketing position and "just loved it." Having learned more about her own motivation and preferences, Susan's next two jobs were pure marketing positions with more autonomy, and exposure to new industries. In each case, however, the payoff for Susan was limited by financial or ownership constraints on what could be done.

Susan was laid off when her employer went bankrupt. After considerable searching, she landed a job with a global company where "all the marketing procedures and everything [are] all really well done" and "where I could learn the proper way to do everything." Susan also reports that "once you've worked for a good company" her reputation in her field has grown considerably. "I've been rung up by quite a few people, headhunting . . . I don't think I'll have much trouble getting a job next time."

In Susan's case, there is an obvious exchange of competence for opportunity in each job she has held. However, the benefits of reciprocity accrue beyond any period of employment: to the meat company in its new recipes and products, to the next three companies in their marketing systems, and to the global company in its product development. Meanwhile the benefits of successive reciprocities to Susan add up to her emergence as a mature and reputable marketing specialist, and a valuable resource to her present and any future company. Reciprocities between companies and employees lead far beyond the realm of near-term satisfaction. They are the building blocks from which both parties engage over time with the economic world.

Taking Benefits Home

Employer–employee reciprocities are not the only ones in which a career actor is involved. The career involves the actor in taking on a series of employment roles, but she or he will also have other roles – for example, parent, family member, and volunteer – each involving other reciprocities. These roles, and their attendant obligations such as caring for children or supporting the community, bring people's career circumstances in contact with a wider set of engagements. This has in the past been a particular issue for women, who tend to take on more demanding responsibilities in the home/family setting.

A concern with reciprocities and larger life activities also invites the question of whether benefits to each contracting party are "bounded" or "boundaryless." Bounded benefits are those which accrue only for the period a job lasts, such as unskilled work for a company in return for wages. Boundaryless benefits are those which endure, such as individual sales experience that gets transferred with a change in employment. In traditional work arrangements, there was (and often still is) a problem with synchronization. Employers would signal reciprocal benefits rather than directly deliver them. They would say "You work for me today; I'll reward your loyalty tomorrow." Such arrangements are frequently structured into formal long-term arrangements such as pension plans and vacation time, as well as into both formal and informal understandings about job security and promotion. However, the implication of weakening situations is that future rewards are less dependable, so that boundaryless benefits become more valuable.[58]

The emergent links among careers, reciprocities, and life beyond work call for a broadening of career theory to better understand and learn from Peter's career and the careers of others. We must acknowledge and include those careers which are not managerial and professional, do not necessarily follow organizational or occupational hierarchies, and are idiosyncratic. We must emphasize the subjective along with the objective career as a necessary focus for understanding. There must be less preoccupation with the "paid-work" component of the career, and more attention to the "unpaid-work" component and family circumstances. Attention needs to be paid to the progressive weakening of employment situations, and the increased opportunity for some individuals to enact their own careers. This is an approach to careers that helps us to understand them not only as phenomena in their own right, but in terms of their enactment of wider social and economic arrangements.

Acting in the Economic Theater

The economic theater – the stage on which we play our parts in working life – is changing. If the Industrial State was theater, it was a centralized, scripted theater, where the producers supplied big production funds, the writers wrote elegant scripts, and the directors coached the cast to perfection on a predetermined plan. The actor's scope was limited. To be selected for the part, he or she had to show some potential, but after that it was largely a matter of learning the writer's lines and following the director's instructions.

As we built our careers, we actors lived out our lives in security, for there usually seemed to be plenty of parts available. But our potential was unfulfilled, since the scripts were often colorless, and the endless repetition of even high-quality performance was undemanding. We tended to become typecast at a younger age than was good for us. Ironically, the more successful the production, the less we developed, for there was nothing new to learn. We could play the same part for years but, when the show closed, we didn't know where to try or how to audition for new parts. And if we found a new part, there was someone else, much more powerful than we were, writing and planning the production, so that again we had nothing to contribute except performing it as directed.

The New Economy, in contrast, is improvisational or street theater. Ideas are decentralized, and can come from anywhere – even from a theatergoer. The boundaries around the roles of "producer," "writer," "director," "actor," "stage manager," "lighting designer" are disappearing. People can use their initiative to take charge. Writers can direct and act in their own productions. Scripts are team-written, loose, and changeable. Drama school and actors' networks celebrate spontaneity ahead of technique and role. Career actors improvise around a mutually-agreed theme, or experiment with a new interpretation. They take on temporary roles in order to learn new skills, work with new people, and then move on.

We have always known, even in the Industrial State, that the knowledge of an enterprise could be retained independently of the specific individuals who contributed. Returning to the theater analogy, we know that Michael Crawford can open in the latest Andrew Lloyd Webber production in New York, and that three years later Michael Crawford will be gone, along with the rest of the original cast, yet the production will be as good as it was on the first night. The expertise of Crawford and the other original cast members has, it seems, been effortlessly transferred to the ongoing production. The limitation, however, is that after three years the script remains unchanged, and there is little margin for improvement. In the New Economy, not only will the cast have changed after three years, but so too will the production, because what the actors bring is not just the clockwork mechanization of a script, but the constant creation of individual and collective novelty.

Our thesis is that as we build our careers, we are all actors. But we are ceasing to be (as we have been encouraged to think) agents for the powerful institutions which try to write our scripts and direct our actions. The scripts of monotonous work, or careful ascent through a series of company job descriptions, or steady specialization in a typecast occupation, or (for women) relegation to the margins of employment because of discontinuities of service, are disappearing. Actors don't like those scripts, because although their parts may be all right for a while, over a lifetime they are essentially one-dimensional and boring. They do not equip us for novel, improvisational parts in the New Theater. Our new skills become less relevant the longer we hold on. Producers find that writing scripts for us no longer works because the market for theater and the technology of theater are changing too quickly: they need actor turnover and freedom from predetermined roles as much as we do.

The Plot of this Book

In this book we take the 75 career actors whom we have interviewed – including Peter and Susan – and report on the roles they have played. We focus on a ten-year period of rapid political and economic change, played out on a world stage involving what many would see as the advent of the New Economy. We present our material in three main parts. The first introduces our topic (this chapter), sketches some preliminary evidence from our research sample (Chapter 2), and presents the main theoretical ideas around which our analysis of careers will be built (Chapter 3). The second part moves through the different kinds of career cycles we have broadly labelled "fresh energy" (Chapter 4), "informed direction" (Chapter 5), and "seasoned engagement" (Chapter 6). The third part aggregates our findings to suggest new ways of thinking about accumulated "career capital" (Chapter 7), and its investment in the institutions of the New Economy (Chapter 8), and explores the future implications of our findings (Chapter 9).

The information presented in the rest of this book could not have been collected from a restricted set of occupations or employer companies. We follow the people, the heroes and heroines of this book, wherever they go. We observe them as they struggle to make sense of their lives, and as they chart their paths within and between jobs, into and out of the workforce, bringing to each new situation fresh insights from their previous experience. Like all of us, they are working to make sense of and influence an environment which dissolves and reforms as it is experienced. What we record is frequently surprising, occasionally delightful, sometimes distressing, but – we believe – always informative. Ours is a story about people preparing for the New Economy through the enactment of their own careers. Our emphasis is on the words of the participants themselves. It is time for those people to be heard.

Notes

1. Arthur, M.B., Hall, D.T. and Lawrence, B.S. (eds.) *Handbook of Career Theory*. Cambridge: Cambridge University Press, 1989, p. 8.

2. For example, Stewart, N. AGTC scores of Army personnel grouped by occupation. *Occupations*, 1947, 26: 5–41.

3. Gutteridge, T.G. Organizational career development systems: the state of the practice. In D.T. Hall and Associates, *Career Development in Organizations*. San Francisco: Jossey-Bass, 1986, pp. 50–94.

4. Betz, N.E., Fitzgerald, N.F. and Hill, R.E. Trait-factor theory: traditional cornerstone of career theory. In Arthur, Hall and Lawrence, op. cit. (1), pp. 26–40; Holland, J.L. *Making Vocational Choices: A Theory of Careers* (2nd ed.), Englewood Cliffs, NJ: Prentice-Hall, 1985.

5. Schein, E.H. *Career Dynamics: Matching Individual and Organizational Needs*. Reading, MA: Addison Wesley, 1978.

6. Weber, M. *The Theory of Social and Economic Organization*. New York: Free Press, 1947.

7. Beer, H.R., Spector, B., Lawrence, P.R., Mills, D.Q. and Walton, R.E. *Human Resource Management*. New York: Free Press, 1985.

8. Wilensky, H.L. Careers, life-styles, and social integration. *International Social Science Journal*, 1961, 12: 553–8.

9. Maslow, A.H. and Chang, H. *The Healthy Personality*. New York, Van Nostrand, 1969; Schein, E.H. *Career Dynamics: Matching Individual and Organizational Needs*. Reading, MA: Addison-Wesley, 1978.

10. Cyntrynbaum, S. and Crites, J.O. The utility of adult development theory in understanding career adjustment processes. In Arthur, Hall and Lawrence, op cit. (1), pp. 66–88.

11. Ornstein, S. and Isabella, L. Age versus stage models of career attitudes of women: a partial replication and extension. *Journal of Vocational Behavior*, 1990, 36: 1–19.

12. Schein, E.H. *Career Anchors: Discovering Your Real Values* (rev. ed.). San Francisco: Jossey-Bass, 1993.

13. Dalton, G. and Thompson, P. The four stages of professional careers. *Organizational Dynamics*, 1977, Summer: 19–42.

14. Kanter, R.M. Careers and the wealth of nations: a macro-perspective on the structure and implications of career forms. In Arthur, Hall and Lawrence, op. cit. (1), pp. 506–22.

15. Arthur, M.B. and Rousseau, D.M. Introduction: the boundaryless career as a new employment principle. In M.B. Arthur and D.M. Rousseau (eds.) *The Boundaryless Career*. New York: Oxford University Press, 1996, pp. 3–20.

16. Whyte, W.H. *The Organization Man*. London: Pelican, 1956.

17. Galbraith, J.K. *The New Industrial State* (2nd ed.). Boston: Houghton Mifflin, 1971.

18. Presthus, R., *The Organizational Society* (2nd ed.). New York: St. Martin's, 1978.

19. Ouchi, W. *Theory Z*. Reading, MA: Addison-Wesley, 1981.

20. Peters, T. and Waterman, R.W. *In Search of Excellence: Lessons from*

America's Best Managed Companies. New York: Harper and Row, 1982; Peters, T. *Thriving on Chaos: Handbook for a Management Revolution.* New York: Knopf, 1987.

21. Burns T. and Stalker, G.M. *The Management of Innovation.* London: Tavistock, 1961.

22. For popular reports see Case, J. *From the Ground Up: The Resurgence of American Entrepreneurship.* New York: Simon and Schuster, 1990; Beck, N. *Shifting Gears: Thriving in the New Economy.* Toronto: Harper, 1995.

23. Quinn, J.B. *Intelligent Enterprise.* New York: Free Press, 1992.

24. Useem, M. Corporate restructuring and the restructured world of senior management. In P. Osterman (ed.) *Broken Ladders: Managerial Careers in the New Economy.* New York: Oxford University Press, 1996, pp. 23–54.

25. Drucker, P.F. *Postcapitalist Society.* New York: HarperCollins, 1993.

26. In this book we refrain from using the term "the organization" to mean an employment entity, to avoid any association with the "organizational society" of old. We use "firm," "company," or "employer," to cover both private and public employment sectors.

27. In Arthur and Rousseau, op. cit. (15), Chapter 1.

28. Barley, S.R., Careers, identities, and institutions. In Arthur, Hall, and Lawrence, op. cit. (1), pp. 41–65.

29. Cressey, P.G. *The Taxi-dance Hall: A Sociological Study in Commercialised Recreation and City Life.* Chicago: University of Chicago Press, 1932. Cited in Barley, op. cit. (28).

30. Bell, N.E. and Staw, B.M. People as sculptors versus sculpture: the roles of personality and personal control in organizations. In Arthur, Hall and Lawrence op cit. (1), pp. 232–52; Bloch, D.P. and Richmond, L.J. (eds.), *Connections Between Spirit and Work in Career Development.* Palo Alto, CA: Davis-Black, 1997.

31. Wheatley, M.J. *Leadership and the New Science.* San Francisco: Berrett-Koehler, 1992.

32. Kiel, L.D. and Elliott, E. (eds.) *Chaos Theory in the Social Sciences: Foundations and Applications.* Ann Arbor, MI: University of Michigan Press, 1996.

33. Arthur, M.B. (ed.) The boundaryless career. Special issue of the *Journal of Organizational Behavior*, 1994, 15 (1): 295–381; Arthur and Rousseau, op. cit. (15).

34. Arthur, M.B. The boundaryless career: a new perspective for organizational inquiry, *Journal of Organizational Behavior*, 1994, 15: 295–306.

35. Fletcher, J.K. and Bailyn, L. Challenging the last boundary: reconnecting work and family. In Arthur and Rousseau, op. cit. (15), pp. 256–67.

36. Saxenian, A.L. Beyond boundaries: open labor markets and learning in Silicon Valley. In Arthur and Rousseau, op. cit. (15), pp. 23–39.

37. Jones, C. Careers in project networks: the case of the film industry. In Arthur and Rousseau, op cit. (15), pp. 58–75.

38. Miles, R.E. and Snow, C.C. Twenty-first century careers. In Arthur and Rousseau, op. cit. (15), pp. 97–115.

39. Arthur, M.B., Claman, P. and DeFillippi, R. Intelligent enterprise, intelligent career. *Academy of Management Executive*, 1995, 9 (4): 7–22.

40. Quinn, J.B. *Intelligent Enterprise.* New York: Free Press, 1992.

41. Kossek, E.E., Huber-Yoder, M., Castellino, D. and Lerner, J. The working poor: locked out of careers and the organizational mainstream. *Academy of Management Executive*, 1997, 11 (1): 76–92.

42. Handy, C.B. *The Empty Raincoat*. London: Hutchison, 1994.

43. Peiperl, M. and Baruch, Y. Back to square zero: the post-corporate career. *Organizational Dynamics*, 1997, Spring: 7–22.

44. Kanter, op. cit. (14).

45. Hirsch, P.M. and Shanley, M. The rhetoric of "boundaryless" – or how the middle class bought into its own marginalisation. In Arthur and Rousseau, op. cit. (15), pp. 218–34.

46. Heckscher, C. *Management Loyalties in an Age of Corporate Restructuring*. New York: Basic Books, 1995.

47. Weick, K.E. *Sensemaking in Organizations*. Thousand Oaks, CA: Sage, 1995, p. 30.

48. Inkson, K. Organization structure and the transformation of careers. In T. Clark (ed.) *Advancements in Organizational Behaviour*. Louth, UK: Ashgate Publishing, 1997.

49. Fondas, N. Feminization at work: career implications. In Arthur and Rousseau, op cit. (15), pp. 282–94.

50. Collin, A. and Watts, A.G. The death and transfiguration of career – and of career guidance? *British Journal of Guidance and Counselling*, 1996, 12 (3): 385–98.

51. Weick, K.E., Enactment and the boundaryless career. In Arthur and Rousseau, op. cit. (15), pp. 40–57; Mischel, W. *Personality and Assessment*. New York: Wiley, 1968.

52. Weick, ibid., p. 44.

53. Ouchi, W. *Theory Z*. Reading, MA: Addison-Wesley, 1981.

54. Saxenian, op. cit. (36).

55. Shipper, F. and Manz, C.C. Employee self-management without formally designated teams. *Organizational Dynamics*, 1992, 20 (3): 48–61.

56. Weick, op. cit. (47), p. 50.

57. Rousseau, D.M. *Psychological Contracts in Organizations*. Newbury Park, CA: Sage Publications, 1995.

58. This applies to boundaryless benefits for the employer, as well, as we will emphasize in Chapter 7.

2 Exploring New Patterns of Career Behavior

Spiralling with Purpose

Catherine completed her undergraduate degree with a specialization in accounting, and continued directly to MBA studies to broaden her credentials. She spent a year as a financial analyst and then moved to a banking job. She earned her professional accountant's certification but realized early on that she wanted to "escape accounting." A positive experience doing part-time tutoring in marketing led her to explore the academic job market. Soon she secured a lecturing position at an institution that was rapidly expanding its business studies programs. Here she learned the theory of marketing ("like being a student again"). Being "thrown in at the deep end," she developed skills of teaching and course organization, and built up her self-confidence. She also developed practical marketing expertise by working on the institution's own marketing of its academic programs. But after four years she was told "You won't get tenure until you do some research." Feeling let down after her years of hard work, Catherine started thinking about career choices. She decided that she was in danger of being "branded an academic" and that, although she loved teaching, "I'd be more credible if I had practical experience."

Through a consultant, Catherine secured a job with a major telecommunications company, and stayed for four years. She moved through four jobs, learning market segmentation and analysis in the first, strategic marketing in the second, advertising and promotion in the third, and pricing and product management in the fourth. These moves involved three relocations: one against the wishes of her boss, because "you had to be in [head office] if you wanted to be involved in the implementation of plans;" one "because I was beginning to get sucked more into the accounting side" instead of more "hands on, producing materials" experience; and one when her husband was relocated and she persuaded the company to relocate her as well.

Next, frustrated because she was not continuing to learn in her fourth company job, and feeling that "I was going to be stuck in telecommunications," Catherine saw a newspaper advertisement for a job as marketing manager of a travel company. She got the job, and for the first time had the experience of managing staff and working across the breadth of the marketing function: "Market research, writing a marketing plan, training up the branches, doing promotions, window displays, everything to do with marketing I had a dabble in. Great experience!" After a year, however, frustrated by a new boss, who "doesn't have a computer on his desk and doesn't practice modern management and knows nothing about marketing," and pregnant with her first baby, Catherine left her job to take some time off and consider the further development of her career.

We begin this chapter with Catherine's story because it features, in microcosm, much of what we have found. Career actors have, most fundamentally, a motivation to work and a willingness to change employers. In pursuit of career exploration and growth they are willing to try new occupations, as Catherine has done three times in the past ten years, or new industries, as she has done four times. They are often willing to relocate – Catherine did so more than once – to take advantage of a fresh opportunity. They may use a second position in paid or unpaid work to open up a new opportunity, as Catherine did through her tutoring efforts. They act idiosyncratically, as when Catherine, the academic, focused on practical marketing instead of research about marketing. They may leverage one job opportunity to obtain another, both between companies (as when Catherine left academia), and within companies (as when Catherine sought new opportunities within the telecommunications company). They adjust career behavior to take account of partners' careers, and they manage issues of balancing work and family.

Catherine's ten-year career history involves more movement than most of the other cases in our sample. However, much that is concentrated in Catherine's story is repeated across the 75 case histories we compiled. She uses her experiences creatively to move away from unattractive base disciplines and to establish good credentials in what comes to be her adopted field. She rotates jobs within a single company, using the company as a kind of customized training-ground for her own personal development. Meanwhile, any ideas her employers may hold that they are developing a loyal employee or a long-term resource are undermined by Catherine's determination to learn and progress on her own terms. These kinds of career patterns and motivations extend across multiple occupational groups in our research sample. The exception – that is, the career that does not conform to the expectations of traditional employment thinking – emerges as the rule in today's employment arena.

About this Study

Our purpose in this study was to gather a set of contemporary "career stories" as a database to enable us to explore and develop common themes and mechanisms covering objective careers, subjective careers, career motivations, job-to-job transitions, and the causal factors perceived to affect career movement and change. We were also interested in the effects of key external stakeholders – partners, families, employers, workmates, unions, professional and trade institutions, and informal networks – on career moves.

We wished to explore the existence and prevalence of concepts associated with boundaryless careers in general,[1] and the enactment of careers in particular,[2] while simultaneously seeking to capture each participant's point of view. We were mindful of the criticisms of traditional career theory (see Chapter 1) which framed careers from a narrow sample base of mainly middle-class white males in specific occupational groups. We set out to avoid such sampling constraints.

To create a sample of career actors broadly representative of the present workforce we used statistical information on gender, ethnic origin, and nine major occupational groups.[3] We excluded people under 25, thereby anticipating at least five years of career experience for all research participants. We excluded retired people. Where potential participants were not currently in the workforce (e.g. women at home with children), we included them if they had been in the workforce during the previous five years or hoped to return to it in the next five.[4] Each participant was assigned a pseudonym.

Our qualitative approach applied general ideas about this kind of research to the particulars of the population we sought to study. Our three main purposes were: to gain a "holistic" sense of the prevailing "context" and "its logic, its arrangements, its explicit and implicit rules" through which careers were acted out; to capture "data on the perceptions of local actors," that is the career actors whom we interviewed in depth; and to explicate ways people "understand, account for, take action, and otherwise manage" their career situations. We sought to grant our research participants the time, the empathy, and the flexibility that would enable them to provide the kind of evidence sought.[5]

The Participants

As already noted, there were 75 case study participants in our sample, spread across nine distinct occupational groups. We set out to draw our sample from within one metropolitan area and the surrounding countryside. Its population was around one million, in an area of around 100 square miles (250 square kilometers). We made random selections from the telephone book, and asked individuals about their work and experience to see if they fitted an available slot in our ideal sample. If they did, and if they met our other criteria, we asked if we could interview them. We could not of course control who decided to accept or decline this request. Many initial telephone contacts – perhaps two-thirds of those we spoke to – declined. However, approximately 50 of the final 75 interviews were arranged by random telephone contact.

When it became apparent that some occupational groups were difficult to reach by the telephone sampling approach, we identified clusters of representative workers and arranged for a random selection to be made on our behalf. For example, an oyster farmer was randomly selected for the "agriculture and fisheries" occupational group from the oyster farmers' association membership rolls. A female, non-Caucasian manager was selected from a list of ethnic high achievers; a welder was selected from one company's group of factory workers. In no case was a person interviewed as a result of direct association with the research team.

Table 2.1 gives details of the members of the sample: pseudonym, gender, age, and occupation at the time of the interview. Where participants were currently not in the workforce, their last position has been used as the basis for classification. Our eventual sample provides a broad cross-section of the nine principal occupational groups.

Table 2.2 summarizes the main features of the sample. The participants included 39 men and 36 women, 61 Caucasians and 14 non-Caucasians. These numbers roughly approximate the gender and ethnic distributions in the national workforce. The ages of participants ranged from 25 to 66, with a median of 42. Again, with the exception of those under 25 with limited career experience, age distribution was fairly represented.

Participants spanned nine occupational groups ranging from top management (group 1) positions to basic jobs such as garbage collector (group 9). As Table 2.2 shows, they were broadly representative of the wider workforce, although slightly over-representative of the "higher" occupational groups. It may be argued the sample is biased toward those who felt, when they heard that our purpose was to explore their career histories, that they had a good story to tell. However, it may also be argued that the sample is biased toward those who were too polite to refuse, or those who wanted to talk because they felt aggrieved about their recent experiences.

Table 2.1   *Research participants and their occupations*

Name	Male/Female	Age	Occupation
Group 1: legislators, administrators and managers			
Catherine	F	33	marketing manager
Cedric	M	47	businessman
Claudia	F	37	chief executive officer
Dan	M	45	landlord
Gareth	M	48	human services manager
Joan	F	34	travel manager
Kirsty	F	30	self-employed retailer
Martin	M	38	company owner
Peter	M	38	managing director
Priscilla	F	27	office manager
Sally	F	32	advertising manager
Group 2: professionals			
Adrian	M	48	research sociologist
Gina	F	29	day care owner/operator
Glenda	F	25	optometrist
Isabel	F	40	research engineer
Janice	F	56	school guidance counselor
Marie	F	50	primary school teacher
Nigel	M	54	church minister
Nita	F	39	secondary school teacher
Oliver	M	53	tutor (college teacher)
Norman	M	54	accountant
Phillip	M	42	town planner
Stephen	M	50	computer consultant
Susan	F	31	product manager
Group 3: technicians and associate professionals			
Albert*	M	26	technical advisor
Barbara	F	47	physical therapist
Elaine	F	56	deputy court registrar
Helen	F	45	nurse
Henry	M	43	computer programmer
Julie	F	26	union organizer
Paula	F	50	office administrator
Quentin*	M	47	air traffic controller
Group 4: clerks			
Anne	F	50	secretary
Christine	F	30	secretary
Elsie	F	46	secretary
Gail	F	45	accounts clerk
Lily	F	32	accounts clerk
Sam	M	41	administrative worker
Vandana	F	25	clerk
Wendy	F	27	secretary

Table 2.1 *(cont.)*

Name	Male/Female	Age	Occupation
Group 5: sales and service workers			
Annette	F	44	cafeteria assistant
Bruce	M	39	salesperson
Damien	M	28	chef/catering manager
Jack	M	26	health assistant
Jennie	F	47	care worker
Jean	F	50	merchandiser
Kelly	F	48	customer service coordinator
Maggie	F	35	restaurant supervisor
Ron	M	58	salesperson
Sargent	M	48	firefighter
Tina	F	55	salesperson (retail)
Group 6: agricultural and fishery workers			
Alex	M	55	farmer
Desmond	M	26	winemaker
Honor	F	43	farmer
Jeff	M	40	landscaper
Owen	M	33	oyster farmer
Tommy	M	34	farm worker
Vera	F	56	orchard farmer
Group 7: trades workers			
Brett	M	32	plasterer
Cliff	M	45	builder
David	M	48	cabinet maker
George	M	51	baker
James	M	51	tiler
Tony	M	34	welder
Group 8: plant and machine operators and assemblers			
Barry	M	29	machine setter
Bert	M	66	driver
Chu	F	27	carpet machine operator
Darren	M	26	truck driver
Jonathan	M	62	factory worker
Group 9: elementary occupations			
Bill	M	39	stagehand
Elisabeth	F	38	cleaner
Evelyn	F	43	warehouse worker
Piers	M	54	storeman
Gus	M	37	stevedore
Troy	M	28	garbage collector

* Albert was originally sampled as a bartender, but upon interview it was discovered he held a day job in engineering.

Quentin received a promotion to manager after he was sampled as an air traffic controller.

Table 2.2 *Overview of the research sample*

Occupation Group	Number	Male	Female	Caucasian	Non-Caucasian	Average age	Age range
Legislators, administrators and managers	11	5	6	9	2	37	27–48
Professionals	13	6	7	12	1	44	25–56
Technicians and associate professionals	8	3	5	6	2	43	26–56
Clerks	8	1	7	6	2	37	25–50
Service and sales workers	11	5	6	9	2	44	26–58
Agricultural and fishery workers	7	5	2	7	0	41	26–56
Trades workers	6	6	0	5	1	44	32–51
Plant and machine operators and assemblers	5	4	1	4	1	42	26–66
Elementary occupations	6	4	2	2	4	40	28–54
Total	75	39	36	60	15	42	25–66

The Process

We usually interviewed participants in their own homes, but at work or elsewhere if they requested it. Most interviews lasted between an hour and an hour and a half. All were, with the participants' agreement, recorded. The interviews were conducted by one member of our team of four, the three authors and a research assistant.[6] The objective of the interview was to build up a comprehensive picture of the participant's work history, particularly the ten-year period just ending. The interview schedule was semi-structured; it included a series of "set" areas of inquiry and a number of set questions. However, participants were encouraged to describe their own histories in their own words.[7]

The interview tapes were transcribed by contract typists. The transcripts were read, analysed, and coded by all three authors. The content analysis covered, for example, voluntary versus involuntary job changes and the circumstances associated with them. It also covered industry, occupation and geographic mobility, participant descriptions of all job changes, as well as reports of the reciprocal benefits participants gave and received for each job they held. The data were transferred to the qualitative analysis computer program

NUD*IST[8] to assist in subsequent analysis. The program was used to record and organize the content analysis, and also as a tool to help develop the kind of descriptive statistics reported later in this chapter.

For further interpretation of the data we relied on direct readings of the transcripts, and cross-checking of our interpretations with other members of the research team. To assist our interpretation we wrote each career up as a "story" – a summary career history, about a page in length, detailing the main features and facts of the career as reported by the participants, plus a brief interpretation. The story was our attempt to capture the unfolding meaning of each person's career from the narrative provided. All of the career stories were written on the basis of the transcript by a researcher other than the one who had conducted the interview.

Each career story was discussed by the research team and adjusted to reflect our shared understanding. In our discussions we tried to be mindful of the cautions to be applied to this kind of work. In particular, we were conscious of the view that "the interpretative practice of making sense of one's findings is both artful and political."[9] We discovered that the artistic and political differences between the members of the research team were substantial, but that talking through our differences gave us a deeper shared understanding of each case.[10] These career stories form the basis of many of the case examples described, though we have frequently returned to the original transcripts in order to add detail.

Employment Mobility and Stability

Although our research method was primarily qualitative, some of the interview material provided us with the opportunity for an initial "broad-brush" quantitative analysis. We offer such an analysis below to provide an overview of the salient features of the data we collected. We refer particularly to the material we gathered on job-to-job transitions. This kind of material has been used elsewhere to map the broad characteristics of career mobility across large samples.[11] It provides a point of departure for the further interpretation we attempt in later chapters.

The thesis we argued in Chapter 1 assumes that present-day careers are characterized by high mobility. In traditional thinking about careers, the general sentiment has been to view mobility as the exception, as something ideally to be avoided by both individuals and companies, as "noise" behind the norm of employment continuity. High mobility has been assumed to be "bad", particularly for companies which have constantly to replace lost skills and experience, but

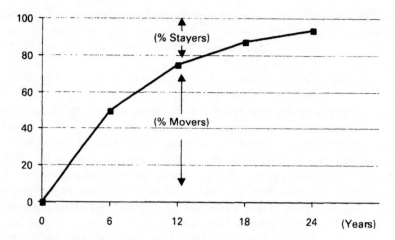

Figure 2.1   *Percentage of movers migrating from the same company as time unfolds (average employment period taken as 6 years)*

also for the individual in terms of insecurity and untapped expertise. If we are to be less tied to the past, either in our assumptions about employment, or in our emotional attachment to the way things used to be, we might usefully revisit these assumptions.

There is increasing evidence that the general sentiment has been misplaced. For example, a study in the UK showed that in 1983 61 percent of a sample of members of the British Institute of Managers had had three or more employers in their career; in a comparable study in 1958, only 24 percent of an equivalent group had had three or more employers.[12] More recently, the median employment period for all U.S. workers was reported to be just four-and-a-half years, and six years for managers.[13] The median employment period for male workers in Japan, supposedly the principal beneficiaries of a system geared to lifetime employment, was recently reported as just eight years;[14] subsequent upheavals in the Japanese economy may have lowered this figure.[15]

The significance of these indicators of relatively rapid mobility is illustrated in Figure 2.1. It shows the dispersion of employees over time given a representative six-year median employment period. Taking this median and projecting forward over twenty years, and assuming people's propensity to change jobs remains constant, we estimate that only 10 percent of a company's employees would still be with the company 20 years later. The remaining 90 percent will have moved on. The picture changes little if we make the assumed employment period longer. For example, with the Japanese male workers cited earlier, an eight-year median employment period means that 75 percent of people will have moved after 16 years, and 88 percent after 24 years. Most people, it seems, move relatively frequently between employers. There is much to be learned from studying why.

Mobility Patterns

The ten-year period of our study was one of rapid political and economic deregulation, and of widespread private and public sector restructuring and downsizing.[16] Our data afforded us the opportunity to study both mobility and stability. We looked particularly at mobility between employers. We also considered mobility in terms of the type and direction of moves that participants made – for example whether such moves resulted in direct career advancement, and whether they crossed the boundaries of industry, occupation, and geographical region.

Sixty of 75 participants changed employer at least once over the ten-year survey period. Three more were self-employed over the full period. Thus, according to a simple definition based on whether they had changed employers or been self-employed over the study period, 84 percent of research participants reflected engagement in boundaryless careers. Those who had not changed employers were five public servants, one minister of religion, one farmer, one accounts clerk, one customer service coordinator, one storeman, one factory worker, and one chronically unemployed person. Over the sample as a whole, mobility emerges as a prominent feature of emerging work arrangements.

The 75 participants held 265 jobs with 217 employers over the ten-year period. In calculating overall statistics for employment mobility, we made adjustments for the truncated job and employment situations reported at the beginning and end of the survey period.[17] Since interviews were collected over a six-month period, we also made adjustments for the overall time employed. Table 2.3 details for each occupational group, the sample as a whole, and the various sub-samples, the average job tenure, employment tenure, total number of layoffs, average length of job tenure, and average length of employment tenure. On the whole, those classed as managers, clerks, and service and sales workers (those whose current job was located by virtue of organizational position) had higher mobility than those whose current job was located by virtue of a profession or trade.

The Merits of Mobility?

Acceptance of an underlying pattern of mobility, or even of potential mobility, raises a new set of questions. Instead of asking, for example,

Table 2.3   *Average job tenure, employment tenure and layoff summary*

Occupation group	Average job tenure (years)	Average employment tenure (years)	Total no. of layoffs	Average no. of jobs[1]	Average no. of employers[1]
Legislators, administrators and managers	3.3	5.8	2[2]	4.5	3
Professionals	6.2	7.5	4[3,5]	2.8	2.5
Technicians and associate professionals	4.1	6	3[4]	3.6	3
Clerks	4	4.8	1	3.9	3.4
Service and sales workers	3.1	4.7	1	4.7	3.4
Agricultural and fishery workers	5.4	6.5	2	3.3	2.9
Trades workers	5	5.4	2[6]	3.2	3
Plant and machine operators and assemblers	6	6	0	2.8	3
Elementary occupations[7]	8.4	9	2[2,3]	2.2	1.7
Total	4.3	5.9	17	3.5	2.9
Males	4.5	6.9	14	3.2	2.5
Females	4	4.8	3	3.9	3.3
Caucasian	4	5.4	14	3.6	3.1
Non-Caucasian	5.6	8.4	3	2.9	2.2

1 The Average No. of Jobs and the Average No. of Employers statistics exclude Bill (long-term disabled) and Elisabeth (sporadically unemployed).
2 Includes a laid-off worker who contracted to do the same work after restructuring.
3 Includes a reported "wrongful dismissal" unrelated to economic circumstances.
4 Includes three layoffs for one young engineer seeking early experience.
5 Includes one layoff negotiated at the worker's insistence.
6 Includes one layoff through occupational injury.
7 These averages are clearly unreliable because of the small sample size.

about "turnover" as a symptom of job dissatisfaction, or of failed management practice, we can ask what price people pay by staying for long periods in the same situation. Do they lose flexibility and versatility? At what point does their ability to contribute to different employment situations begin to be reduced? And what of their employing company? When and how much does people's continued tenure block the possible acquisition of innovative newcomers?

We can also ask about the learning process. How does mobility contribute to individual learning over time? How does individual learning contribute to company learning as people move between employment situations? What are the consequences of learning relationships that span the boundaries between companies rather than being restricted by them? More broadly, how do people exercising boundaryless career behavior contribute to the unfolding fabric of the New Economy?

Another feature of our sample is one of relative job stability. The average job tenure period, adjusting for periods of unemployment and incomplete jobs at the start and end of the survey period, is almost four-and-a-half years. The average employment period in any company is almost six years. These figures include all layoffs, which average less than two per year across all 75 participants. At least three of these layoffs were negotiated to the mutual benefit of both employer and employee, as in the case of Peter (Chapter 1). Among the 60 people who reported a change of employer, the average job period was still close to four years and the average employment period close to five years. Although there are wide variations on either side of these averages, they do suggest that typical employment arrangements provide a substantial time for employer and employee to get to know and deliver value to each other. Job moves, even in a period of relatively rapid restructuring, appear overall to be far from whimsical.

Upwards or Sideways?

Our data on job transitions also enabled us to look at the types of move that participants made. From their commentaries on each transition, which typically involved explaining the rationale for moving and the nature, level, and location of the new job, we were able to classify job moves in two ways: whether they showed evidence of normative career advancement in terms of greater responsibility or status, or better pay; or whether they involved change to a new occupation, and/or industry, and/or geographical location.

Considering the prevalence of the "onward-and-upward" model of careers in public consciousness, it is perhaps surprising that most voluntary job changes did not involve career advancement (Table 2.4). Further, most reported cases of conventional career advancement occurred between companies (22 percent of all job changes) rather than within companies (15 percent). This is despite the further observation that half of the moves between companies did not involve traditional career advancement at all. Even though all research participants faced a reportedly rapid pace of economic change, involuntary changes were relatively rare (9 percent of all job changes). Finally, as the above data already suggest, the proportion of inter-company job changes (79 percent) greatly exceeds that of intra-company job changes (21 percent). Most movement in most people's careers occurred between companies, rather than between jobs within companies.

Table 2.4 *Frequency and direction of inter-company and*
intra-company job changes

	No. of people	No. of moves	% of total moves (of 192)
Inter-company moves			
Career advancement	29	43	22
Other, voluntary	48	95	50
Involuntary	11	14	7
Subtotals	59	152	79
Intra-company moves			
Career advancement	19	29	15
Other, voluntary	7	8	4
Involuntary	3	3	2
Subtotals	21	40	21
All job moves			
Career advancement	39	72	38
Other, voluntary	54	103	54
Involuntary	14	17	9
Totals	64	192	100

New Career Directions

Another interesting feature of the data concerns the frequency of new career directions involving changes in industry or occupation, or geographic moves (Table 2.5). All of these are relatively common-place in inter-company moves, with similar frequencies of moves to a new industry (33 percent) or a new occupation (33 percent), and moves to a new geographic location (29 percent) not far behind. In only 5 percent of inter-company moves did industry, occupation, and location remain the same. In contrast, new career directions through intra-company moves were relatively rare. The implication is that those who are mobile between employers usually take on more than one kind of change since they typically change industry and/or occupation and/or geographic location as well. If versatility is, as we believe, an increasingly important attribute for the career actor, this is an important factor.

Another source of career stability is occupation. Our evidence suggests that occupational roles were often constant, and therefore a likely stabilizing influence, for the majority of our participants. Out of 75 members, we counted 31 (41 percent) as having been working in the same general occupation throughout the ten years covered. (In the case of those whose careers had not yet covered ten years, we counted from the start of their first "career" job.) Only one of these

Table 2.5   *Job changes involving a change in industry, occupation, or geographic location*

	No. of people	% of people (of 75)	No. of moves	% of moves (of 143)
Inter-company moves				
Change in industry	31	41	48	33
Change in occupation	32	42	47	33
Change in geographic location	21	28	41	29
Subtotals	40	53	136	95
Intra-company moves				
Change in industry	0	0	0	0
Change in occupation	5	7	5	4
Change in geographic location	2	3	5	3
Subtotals	6	8	10	7
All job moves				
Change in industry	31	41	48	34
Change in occupation	37	49	52	36
Change in geographic location	23	31	43	30
Totals	42	56	143	100

showed any immediate signs of moving to something different. A further 11 (15 percent) had been in the same general occupation for at least the previous five years. As expected, remaining in the same occupation was related to age and gender, with older workers and male workers more likely to be in the same occupation (Table 2.6).

Cycling and Spiralling

The data on mobility call into question the stereotype of movement in careers as typically occurring within organizational or occupational "chimneys" which both confine and channel career movements. The typical job-to-job moves exemplified by our data are characteristically non-linear. The career actor may make lateral, diagonal, or apparent downward shifts to adapt to a changing situation. In any case, as structures flatten, and networked, project, and flexible forms multiply, terms such as "upward" and "downward" lose meaning. As we have seen, the career actor may change not just employer, but industry, occupation, and geographical location as well. Idiosyncratic movement may arise from individual action or be precipitated through collective actions. Career actors "cycle" around activities without apparent progression, or "spiral" around different activities so that some progression is apparent in terms of personal fulfillment, learning, or earnings.

Table 2.6 *Participants working in the same occupation*

Group	Number	Number and % in same occupation at end of 10 years
Age 25–35	26	6 (31%)
Age 37–47	26	12 (45%)
Age 48–66	23	13 (59%)
Male	39	18 (46%)
Female	36	13 (36%)

In considering this phenomenon we have found it useful to draw on the work of Judi Marshall.[18] According to Marshall, career actors do not cycle only around achievements and jobs. Cycles and spirals integrate our social roles as workers in the economic system with our personal identities and needs, and our other roles as family and community members. We may cycle from controlled action to "letting go," or from learning on the job to learning through parenting and child-rearing. According to Marshall,[19] any lack of objective career movement should not be seen as a plateau: rather we need to value such apparent stagnation as "incubation or regeneration." In linear career thinking, such "time out" from careers makes an uneasy fit with conventional expectations of career progress. Marshall links this unease to the principle of linear progression symbolized in mythology as the arrow. In contrast, the principle of development is represented by a spiral and is associated with "space and a more cyclic pattern of change and transformation."[20] She suggests that such a cyclic model is "based on notions of ebb and flow, of shedding and renewal . . . [which] involve giving something up, letting achievements go . . . [and] requires considerable faith that future creativity will be possible."[21]

Cycling in a career means moving in and out of different realms of activity. In addition to changes of employment, industry, occupation, and location, examples include changing the job itself, moving between projects, moving between full-time and part-time work, moving between work commitments and family commitments. In cycling there is little sense of direct progression or increase in formal achievement. However, the same moves may be more rewarding: in "spiralling," the career actor moves through different arenas with a strong undercurrent of personal learning and development.

Cyclic and spiral career behavior takes place in a context of "communion" with the environment (see Chapter 3). It is enhanced by self-understanding, faith in the environment to provide opportunity, and confidence that the career actor will be able to enact new opportunities. Traditional bounded careers, originally configured by the work lives of men, and symbolized by the arrow, progress in an upward linear fashion. Changing roles for women and men, and the rapidly altering external work environment, loosen the gendered associations of arrows and cycles. Boundaryless careers flow and change, cycle between employers and between work and non-work realms of activity. These cycles of change are accelerating.[22]

A Paradox

This chapter has reported a remarkable paradox: participants report a strong pattern of relative job stability within a larger context of persistent career mobility. Most career actors perform one job for a considerable time, but take their next job with a different employer. Moreover, most frequently, the next job represents a lateral move rather than orthodox career advancement. Most career moves take place across company boundaries. Moreover, this brings with it a high frequency of movement across occupational, industrial, and geographical boundaries as well. There is an emergent message of accumulation and transfer of job skills across, rather than within, employment boundaries. The patterns observed suggest the greater relevance of a spiral, rather than a linear, image of career progression.

Our opening chapter's conception of the actor in the economic theater now appears as something of a wandering troubadour. The troubadour moves from company to company, gains fresh experience, shares talents with others, and then moves on. To help us understand the troubadour better, we now explore some theory.

Notes

1. Arthur, M.B. and Rousseau, D.M. *The Boundaryless Career*. New York: Oxford University Press, 1996.

2. Weick, K.E. Enactment and the boundaryless career: organizing as we work. In Arthur and Rousseau, op. cit. (1), pp. 40–57.

3. *New Zealand Standard Industrial Classification of Occupations*. Wellington, N.Z.: Department of Statistics, 1990.

4. In applying these criteria and collecting the relatively large number of 75 case studies, we were seeking "reliability" in our data in the sense that they were "independent of accidental circumstances of the research." (Kirk, J. and Miller, M.L. *Reliability and Validity in Qualitative Research*. Thousand Oaks, CA: Sage, 1986.)

5. All quotations are from Miles, M.B. and Huberman, A.M. *Qualitative Data Analysis*. Thousand Oaks, CA: Sage, 1994, pp. 6–7.

6. Research assistant Karen O'Shea conducted twelve interviews.

7. The full interview protocol is available from the authors.

8. *User's Guide for QSR NUD*IST*. Thousand Oaks, CA: Sage/Scolari, 1995.

9. Denzin, N. and Lincoln, Y. (eds.) *Handbook of Qualitative Research*. Thousand Oaks: Sage Publications, 1994, p. 15.

10. The benefits of using multiple researchers are noted in Eisenhardt, K.M. Building theories from case study research, *Academy of Management Review*, 1989, 14 (4): 532–50, and Yin, R.K. *Case Study Research: Design and Methods*. Thousand Oaks, CA: Sage, 1989.

11. Nicholson, N. and West, M. *Managerial Job Change: Men and Women in Transition*. Cambridge: Cambridge University Press, 1988; Inkson, K. The effects of economic recession on managerial job change and careers. *British Journal of Management*, 1995, 6: 185–95.

12. Nicholson and West, op. cit. (11), pp. 46–7.

13. Maguire, S.R. Employer and occupational tenure: an update. *Monthly Labor Review*, 1993, June: 45–56.

14. Cheng, M.T. The Japanese employment system. *Work and Occupations*, 1991, 18 (2): 148–71.

15. McCarthy, T. Japan's elegant suicide. *Time*, 15 Feb., 1999.

16. Kelsey, J. *The New Zealand Experiment*. Auckland: Auckland University Press, 1995. Russell, M. *Revolution: New Zealand from Fortress to Free Market*. Auckland: Hodder Moa Beckett, 1996.

17. We made the statistical assumption that on average incomplete jobs at the beginning and end of the survey period would last for twice the period reported. We made a similar assumption for incomplete employment periods. Where only one job or employer covered the full survey period, we doubled that period. Since our interview asked people to describe their career histories "since the beginning of 1985," and since we interviewed most research participants in the second half of 1995, we have taken the duration of the survey period to be 10.75 years.

18. This section is based on Marshall, J. Re-visioning career concepts: a feminist invitation. In M.B. Arthur, D.T. Hall and B.S. Lawrence (eds.) *Handbook of Career Theory*. Cambridge: Cambridge University Press, 1989, pp. 275–91.

19. ibid., p. 284.

20. ibid., p. 280.

21. ibid., p. 285.

22. Weick, op. cit. (2), pp. 50–1.

3   Enactment in Career Behavior

Taking Charge

Gus left school at 15, without qualifications, and quickly found a position at a local process factory. In his first week, he met Willie and Kevin, who were as new as he was, and became his friends. Over the next 20 years, Gus and his friends worked in every job in the factory that had little skill requirement: lifting and carrying, clearing and cleaning, working in the warehouse. Latterly they worked mainly in the loading gangs which handled the large-scale deliveries of the company's raw materials. After 16 years' total service, Gus was made foreman on the loading gang: "I think they offered me the job to get me away from the union." There was paperwork involved and although Gus no longer had to do manual work, he did: "I wanted to do the same as the other people did."

Then came change – new management, a leaner, meaner structure. The company had to remain competitive. Gus was told that the loading gangs would have to go. The company believed it could get the job done more cheaply by contracting it out. Gus understood this, as well as the employment system underlying the problem: "They didn't think we were productive enough and in a way they were right . . . We got paid when there was a ship in. . . . The longer the ship was in the more we were paid . . . so there was no incentive to go faster." In the end, the failing employment system brought a good layoff package for Gus and his workmates, based on their years of service. They were still young and fit enough to look for work elsewhere, when, along with 27 other loaders, they were laid off.

On the evening of their last day at work Gus, Willie and Kevin got together in the pub. They cajoled each other into putting in a bid for the loading contract. They weren't businessmen, but they reckoned they knew the work as well as anyone. Gus's wife had a typewriter. They found some fancy-looking note paper, invented a company name for themselves, and sent in a quote for the loading work for the next two years. They were astonished to receive an almost immediate reply from the company expressing strong interest in their quote and inviting them for interview. Gus thought the interview would be the end of the matter, when the company realized who they really were.

But the interviewer was one of the new managers, who hadn't met them before. His only concern was to try to get them to provide a quote for five years rather than two. However, Gus, Willie, and Kevin put their heads together and decided they'd rather sign for two years, drive up the price through good performance, and then renegotiate. A two-year contact was signed.

Now, it's nearly two years on and business is going well. Gus still does some manual work, but now much of his time is spent recruiting and supervising gangs, and administering his contract. The manual work takes, on average, one week in four. He takes home the same amount of money as he used to, but also leaves a substantial amount in the business. He has a lot more free time, and spends much of it in youth work and sports coaching. His company is beginning to be sought out for other loading contracts - "but we like it the way it is at the moment, you don't have to work all the time." He is considering diversification into new lines of business such as cleaning.

Not all Gus's ex-workmates have been so fortunate. Some are still unemployed, depressed, and bitter about their experience. Gus has good contacts with them, and employs them on his gangs when he can. He says he gives work to young people who would otherwise be "robbing my house." Gus has been individually enterprising, but he feels a responsibility to others, and, to the best of his ability, he shares the fruits of his enterprise in his local community.

Gus says that sending in the quote to his ex-employer was a practical joke. If it was, then Gus's change in status was largely unanticipated good luck. But some might suspect that Gus and his friends were in fact being more enterprising than they cared to admit. Gus, the unskilled employee, whose working life was acted out at the direction of his company and his trade union, has, in one stroke, effected a remarkable career transition. He has taken charge of his own life instead of letting it continue to be directed by others. He has gone from "working stiff" to "businessman." Rather than having his career determined by the company, he is using his career to joint-venture with the company while at the same time creating his own new company. Who says companies shape careers? Gus's company used to shape his career, but now his career shapes companies.

Gus is a career actor. His working life is a performance on the economic stage. But now, instead of responding to a company script and company direction, he writes his own script and directs his own action. But he does so, not as a classic stand-alone entrepreneur, but as a collaborative actor/director acutely aware of, and connected to, his past and his social experience of work. His knowledge of his company's operations, and his friendship with Willie and Kevin, are critical both to his contribution to the script, and to his performance in his new role. Gus, we submit, is typical of the "knowledge worker" associated with the New Economy.

Enactment

Gus's taking control over his own career, and in turn over his life, his colleagues, his company, and the economy in which he operates, represents a prime example of what Karl Weick calls *enactment*.[1] From Weick's standpoint (briefly introduced in Chapter 1), the career is, in part, the person's own creation. The career is not defined by a series of occupational classifications, rules of professional practice, and progress, or company-based systems of human resource development or succession. These are relevant, of course, but equally important is the individual's own exertion of will in choice and activity. The person enacts the career, and, equally importantly, the career enacts much of the environment in which the career takes place. Think less of the company as a set of environmental forces determining the person's career; think rather of the company as a dynamic nexus of interacting career behaviors, including those of the owners. Gus's previous union-centered career behavior contributed to the downfall of the old employment system. Then, as the labor element of the factory was outsourced, Gus typed a letter and created a new company in which to redefine both his own career and those of others.

The basis of enactment is the imposition of individual will in situations where choice is possible. Weick argues that as workplace boundaries dissolve and bureaucracies weaken, there is greater scope for individuals to exercise choice in their individual behavior. But individual behavior is not arbitrary or anarchic, nor is it alienated from the person's social setting and past. On the contrary, as in Gus's case, the person's accumulated experience and knowledge, family and social networks, and economic connections, powerfully mediate and facilitate the choices that he or she makes. Moreover, as we also noted in Chapter 1, the tendency of post-industrial society is to create progressively "weak" situations – that is, situations of ambiguity, with few guides to action.[2] It follows that individual action is likely to be increasingly derived from individual choice.

Gus's story demonstrates several features of the enactment of career behavior which will become integral to the shifting self-organizing landscapes of the New Economy. Gus gave himself choice by leveraging his experience, his skills, and his social networks. Almost unconsciously, over the first 20 years of his career he had acquired economically relevant learning and had made investments which he was able to turn into valuable intellectual and social capital.

Stories

As we enact our careers, we create "stories." A career story is a personal "moving perspective" on who we are and what we are able to do.[3] It incorporates both the subjective career and the objective career. We create stories retrospectively, interpreting into a coherent picture the fragments that make up our career experience. We seek to provide ourselves with identity and direction, and to signal to others who we are, what we are able to do, and how we might help them. A career story is based on the events, such as job moves and job titles, of the objective career, but also includes memories of subjective career phenomena such as satisfactions, emotions, and ambitions. The story is unwritten (except as it emerges in formal c.v.s) and usually unspoken (except when explicitly requested, as in a job interview or in the research protocol of this study). The story aids comprehension of, and response to, career-relevant stimuli such as current job characteristics and new opportunities.

In passing, and in anticipation of later material in this book, we note a distinction between stories and "scripts." Scripts are institutionally rather than individually determined programs, which "encode contextually appropriate behaviors and perceptions" and "are plans for recurrent patterns of action that define, in observable terms, the essence of actors' roles."[4] Career-influencing scripts may come from the employing company with its scripts of hierarchical or functional ascent, from professional or industry interests with their scripts of focused expertise, or from family and social contexts with their scripts of gender-based division of labor, secure economic platforms for family life, or entrepreneurial accumulation of capital. Scripts may be woven into the fabric of career stories, providing unconscious stereotypes as a basis for self-judgement. The interplay between the institutional script and the personal story provides the career with much of its dynamics and direction.

The story moves in fits and starts, sometimes ascending a pre-planned path, sometimes laboring in a rut or on a plateau as experience is built, at other times veering tangentially in unexpected directions, doubling back on itself for a fresh start, or taking time out for reflection and future planning. Careers, and therefore stories, have continuities and discontinuities. The problem is that because of our acceptance of the Industrial State and structured, hierarchical bureaucracies, we tend to look to our careers for upwardly-directed continuity, represented by such phrases as "climbing the ladder," and "getting to the top." Discontinuity is judged as uncommitted and disruptive. Thus, a person who abandons a conventional career for something quite new is expected to "go back to Square One." A woman who leaves the job to spend a few years bringing up a family full-time is assumed to have abandoned her career or placed it in limbo. At school, careers advisors talk of careers in a language of lifelong, single-occupation or single-industry chunks: for example "a career in nursing" or "a career in banking." Yet, most of the stories of the career-makers whom we interviewed typically showed variety and mobility beyond these stereotyped structures.

For example, take the stories of Priscilla and Gina, both in their late twenties.

Company Utility Player

Priscilla left school at 17. She wanted to build her career as a designer, and soon joined an interior design company as a trainee designer. But she learned multiple skills quickly and was promoted to designer and then to senior designer. The company expanded and she was asked by her boss to take on the job of contracts manager, liaising with customers and subcontractors. When a recession hit and the company downsized, Priscilla took on extra duties as others left the company, and became office manager, adding to her repertoire new skills mostly far removed from her original design interests. Ten years into her career, she is still with her original employer. She and a colleague, with the blessing of the owner, solicit all new business, build client relations, run the office, maintain the books, and even decide their own pay.

Priscilla's identity is a cross between "loyal company servant" and "enterprising business professional." She identifies strongly with the company, and prides herself on excellence at every job in the office. Yet the lists of acquired skills that she reels off, and the client base she has built, are not necessarily company-specific. She has become an accomplished designer and business person with transferable skills and a portable network. She is married and would like to have children and hopes the company will negotiate to let her work part-time, at least temporarily. When the moment for that negotiation comes, one can imagine the company needing her more than she needs the company.

Moving up, Moving on

Gina was a factory worker, but the husband and wife who owned the factory noticed that she had a special facility with children. They would ask her to look after their children in the park instead of doing her factory job. They said she shouldn't be in a factory, she should be working with children. They wrote her a glowing reference. Gina bluffed her way into an interview and took on a difficult commute and a 40 percent drop in wages to become a day-care worker. She already knew that she had, albeit accidentally, found the occupation she wanted. The employer supported her training to qualify as a supervisor, but then promoted a less qualified person to a vacant supervisor's position. Gina left and got a supervisory position elsewhere.

Eventually Gina was dismissed after a disagreement with her boss. But nine of the parent-customers of the facility sided with Gina in the dispute, and urged her to set up her own center. She did so, and it has grown substantially. Gina is strongly committed to her industry, and takes a strong advocacy role within it, including extensive networking with other child-care providers. She plans to start her own family soon, and with her highly supportive husband, looks forward to taking more and more of a manager's rather than a direct carer's role. Ten years on from her original job as a factory worker, Gina reflects how she was originally "almost pathetic, shy and quiet." Now, through taking on more responsibility with each experience, Gina has become an enterprising businesswoman and a passionate advocate for child care.

Thus, in a short period, Priscilla built herself into an indispensable "utility player" who nevertheless had multiple transferable skills on which to base her career development should her company collapse. The employer–employee reciprocities described in Chapter 1 are strong, yet it is likely that Priscilla would be able to carry the benefits she has obtained from her employer into new employment. Gina went from "factory worker" to "child care worker" to "child care supervisor" and "child care professional' to "business owner," "child care advocate," perhaps even "entrepreneur." Whereas Priscilla's career has been built around a particular employer, the central theme of Gina's is occupation or industry. Yet both careers show an unfolding dynamic which makes "employer" or "occupation" inadequate as a means of understanding where the person now stands.

The two stories have much in common with each other, as they do with many of the stories told by members of our sample. The commonalities point to further themes in the enactment of careers, themes about the two-way influence between people and their work environments.

1 Stories include substantial elements of self-directed *improvisation*. Stories do not emphasize predetermined plans stemming from either the career actor or the employer. Rather, people extemporize spontaneously, enacting fresh choices in response to changing circumstances.

2 Stories reflect exercises in retrospective *sensemaking*. People act, reflect on, and make sense of their actions with the benefit of hindsight. To paraphrase Karl Weick's oft-repeated aphorism,

they "only know what they think when they see what they say" about what they have done.[5]

3 There is a cumulative pattern of *adaptation*. New experiences build on previous ones, and in the process people either confirm or disconfirm interpretations of what has gone before. With new experiences, people may see new patterns in, and make new sense of, their earlier career behavior.

4 A primary motive underlying stories is persistent *learning*. People accumulate learning as a principal career-relevant resource, maintain it through changes in the structure of their employing companies or through transitions to new situations, and use it to ensure ongoing readiness for future opportunities.

5 Career behaviors enacted into stories may be expressions of *agency*, involving the pursuit of independence and autonomy, or of *communion*, involving the nurturing of relationships and connectedness. Most career stories are mediated by elements of both agency and communion.

Improvisation

Much long-term career development is based on people acting in ways which career manuals describe as a poor basis for long-term decision-making. Careers are a primary basis for economic well-being or relative poverty, or for deep fulfillment or unimaginable frustration. With so much at stake, career choices and changes should be taken seriously. Yet people make changes when they are under pressure (for example, unemployed), and have poor information. Or they make changes light-heartedly, as an almost playful experiment. Or they pick up on a passing opportunity because there will be no second chance. Many of the choices are not easily reversible.

In considering improvisation, we can make an interesting parallel between careers and music. Gioia[6] in his essay on the nature and history of jazz, describes the impact of the great improvisational trumpet player Louis Armstrong. When Armstrong joined the influential Fletcher Henderson band in 1924, jazz was tamer and more scripted than it was to become. Armstrong was a poor reader of music (in our terms the "script"), but he made up for this limitation by his startlingly energetic and original improvisations (in our terms the "story"). Skillful improvisation became the fashion in jazz as other musicians sought to emulate Armstrong, imprinting their own interpretations on basic themes and moving always onwards, developing the music and not repeating it. In improvisation, the performer is composer, but the composition is gone as soon as it is created, for it is not written down. Gioia contrasts Armstrong's vibrant, memorable improvisations with another fashion of the day – "furniture music" – seamless background music stripped of emotional content, there as environment, the precursor of Musak.

Career actors may be furniture musicians, accepting career forms composed and scripted in corporations and associations, or solo artists jamming joyfully (or anxiously) in the ongoing composition and dissolution of their own lives. Playing corporate furniture music may provide opportunities for virtuosity, or the pleasure of collective involvement in an aesthetic activity, or the secure familiarity of a backdrop which makes few challenges. Improvising one's career brings greater opportunities for novel learning, but also higher risks that one's solos will be boring and tuneless. The familiar structures of organization and occupation encourage us to believe that (mass-produced) furniture careers are the only ones available. The dissolving architecture of great corporations challenges improvisers to blow their horns.

But improvisation does not mean formlessness. Nor does it mean composing great work from scratch. Armstrong's great improvisations needed the basic forms of "Shanghai Shuffle," "Struttin' with some Barbecue," and "West End Blues" as anchors, perhaps in the same way as Schein identifies "career anchors" – enduring clusters of values, interests, and experiences – as structures around which contrasting career episodes are assembled into a whole, integrated form. As jazz players cycle and recycle, providing constant new experiences through the creative redevelopment of past themes, career actors spiral their ways into new industries, occupations, and opportunities, still utilizing basic competencies and accumulating more advanced ones as they go.

There were many examples of improvised behavior in our career stories. A clerk saw a television program that inspired her to visit the local law courts to look for work; a 20-year career in the courts followed. Every few years, the court worker engineered a change of department or location to provide a new set of challenges. A stock exchange worker walked out of his job in anticipation of a stock crash, took a plastering job for a few days to tide himself over, and ended up plastering, and liking it, for years. But plastering, initially an improvised novelty for which he had had no formal training, soon became his "furniture" career, the backdrop for his more improvisational forays into performance in music, theater, and film.

Sensemaking

In the era of the Industrial State it was fashionable to talk about planning – national planning, corporate planning, and at the individual level "career planning" – to pursue orderly progress towards previously determined goals. However, it has become clear that the virtues of planning were overstated. For example, the potter does not "plan" the detail of what he or she will make in advance. Rather, a potter's hands gradually shape a piece of clay into an artistic work. The potter has only a vague conception of how the item will be when complete. The ongoing process ties together the lived experience of a raw lump of clay becoming a half-fashioned article, and a generalized sense of the future possibilities the unfinished article suggests.[7]

Similarly, as Gioia points out, jazz is retrospective: "The improviser may be unable to look ahead to what he is going to play, but he can look behind at what he has just played."[8] The way potters and jazz musicians make sense of their unfolding artistry suggests much about how people make sense of their careers. More than the single pot or the impromptu jazz performance, the career must make sense to its actor as it unfolds. The career is less about a planned destination than it is about a series of lived experiences along the way. Career actors may not have a good sense of where they are going, but they can interpret remarkably well the pattern of their previous career episodes and use this pattern as a basis for fresh choice.

Making sense of employment and other institutional environments is an important human activity. The sense which we make of situations is often dependent on the actions we take in response to them, rather than the other way round. Careers are particularly susceptible to retrospective sensemaking because in essence careers – as replayed in the career actors' minds, or in their responses to our interview questions – are narratives. Thus:

> People who build narratives of their own lives use hindsight. Typically they have access to some felt outcome that can guide them retrospectively as they search for an efficient causal chain capable of producing that feeling. Stories are inventions rather than discoveries.[9]

Both Priscilla and Gina built the narratives of their respective careers. Priscilla wanted to get into design work, but had only a vague idea of what that work entailed. Gina had no intention of working in childcare until her talents in that area were pointed out to her. Each stumbled into a situation with potential: Priscilla into a flexible, informal company where she could experiment with different skills and roles, Gina into an industry which felt right in terms of the sense that she was beginning to make of her own past. After that they built the narratives of their separate careers. Responding to unforeseen events such as the downsizing of Priscilla's company and Gina's dismissal from her supervising job, they have each developed their careers through interpretation of a turbulent past in which long-term plans could not be made. They have made retrospective sense of their careers and ascribed themselves identities from which to look out for their careers ahead.

Adaptation

Careers, like any long-term patterns, can be viewed as sequences of fragmentary events. Some of these events are predictable on-the-job actions and interactions, others are adaptive responses or spontaneous contributions to the constantly unfolding situation. Within jobs, the challenge to adaptation may come from a new technology grappled with and mastered, a stimulating conversation with a colleague or customer, a flash of recognition – *This is (or isn't) what I really want*. Between jobs, the stimulation may be a period of depression or reflection or elation, an unusual job advertisement suddenly noticed in the paper, a chance meeting with "a friend of a friend." Often, the fragments seem, in themselves, ridiculously tiny to bear the weight of many years of the person's subsequent life experience: for example, Gus's practical joke in the pub, Priscilla's agreement to take on an office role as her company downsized, Gina's being fired for expressing her feelings too freely.

But "improvised work experiences that rise into fragments prospectively . . . fall into patterns retrospectively, a mixture of continuity and discontinuity."[10] Few careers appear planned. Rather, we juggle past experiences, present realizations and opportunities, and vague inclinations about the future. We act spontaneously to survive in a harsh world, to learn, to experiment, to confirm or develop our identities. We seldom know, really, where we are going, yet when we get there, we can make good sense of the unfolding pattern. Although we never set the goal, it seems, with the benefit of 20/20 hindsight, that we always had it. What we experience is nothing so predictable as achieving a career objective. Rather, it is what Bateson calls a "triumph of adaptation."[11] For example:

Breaking with the Past

Bruce trained as a boilermaker. He never finished his apprenticeship, but learned to "sort of bulldoze my way into jobs." For over 15 years he followed the work available in his trade around construction sites, project to project, suffering some health damage as a result of his work. He enjoyed the strongly bonded male culture of itinerant boilermaker work, and the strong ethos of trade unionism. He was a union official. "We took on some pretty big companies, and brought them to their knees a few times." But eventually he disagreed with the union's policies, and began to be ostracized by his co-workers. When he was laid off, there was no one to help him. He tried temporary work, laboring and supervising juvenile offenders on simple land-clearing. Then, desperate for a change, he phoned an overseas friend who owned a resort hotel, and she invited him to come over and work in the bar. He took up the offer, but within a few weeks of his arrival the resort went into receivership. Distressed, Bruce thought he would quickly be looking for manual work again, but . . . "the receiver said, 'I've been watching you for the last three weeks and I'm offering you the job of Duty Manager' . . . I just couldn't believe they'd offer me that, but they'd come in and they had seen that I was honest, watching me work the (cash registers) and that, and they needed somebody who didn't have any bad habits."

Bruce was Duty Manager for a year. He learned people skills, book-keeping and budgeting. He returned home and used his new-found people skills to get a job in a used car dealership. In that job he developed further skills in making and closing sales, which he in turn used to blend with his old boilermaking skills to land a job as an engineering supplies representative. Bruce is now a trusted confidant of the company's owner, and an active contributor the company's strategic direction.

For years Bruce defined himself as a manual worker, strong trade unionist, and "buddy" of his fellow union members. A combination of economic pressures and his own maturing values tossed him out of his niche into an unforgiving world. A series of chances – a call to a former acquaintance, a company bankruptcy, an observant and sympathetic receiver – gave him an unexpected opportunity, and Bruce seized it.

Learning

Bruce's case is not only about adaptation, however, it is also about learning. Learning is a central feature of reciprocities with employers, and of employer-to-employer moves, for the successful career actor. In the New Economy, those who thrive will be the knowledgeable and the adaptable, those who have learned from the past, and those who have learned how to learn from the future.[12] Learning drives one's readiness for future learning in a virtuous cycle of new opportunities.

The theme of ongoing learning was powerful not only in the careers of those such as Gus, Gina and Peter (Chapter 1) who capitalized on employment experiences to launch their own self-employed ventures. Learning was prominent in the careers of most members of our sample who, like Priscilla, achieved reasonable career success in employed positions. Consider, for example, the career of Damien.

Cooking with gas

Damien quickly became bored with his formal auto glazing apprenticeship and got a job as a kitchen hand, working his way up through a combination of experience and formal training to become a skilled chef. For several years he worked mainly in one hotel, to which he remained loyal. But "from time to time I would leave and go and get experience elsewhere . . . I wanted as much knowledge as I could." His home hotel had only à la carte service, so he spent some time in another hotel to learn buffet work. Other hotels had different styles of cuisine and service, and he would join specifically to learn the new skills. Within his home hotel he would volunteer for novel work. To learn both technical and managerial skills he watched the work of the role model chefs he worked under. But as his expertise and seniority increased, so came problems of stress. Damien became arrogant and demanding, and went through one period where he had eight jobs in two years: "I would have disagreements with management . . . when we couldn't agree I would walk out." Damien reports that he "had a nervous breakdown" before following his wife's advice to take a stress management course, "one of the best things I ever did." He and his wife then went abroad and ran the kitchen in an Olde English pub, before returning home where he obtained a job as the second chef of a large restaurant. He has since been promoted to head chef, and looks forward to moving to restaurant management or possibly his own franchise or restaurant. He is 28.

Damien's career has been dedicated to learning, accomplished by rapid job-to-job moves, and experiences chosen for their diversity within a common occupational framework. While his technical learning has been the most apparent, he has also learned about management and about himself. His unfolding career can be viewed as a "repository of knowledge."[13] Learning is the means of building and replenishing the stock of knowledge, which includes not just technical and administrative skills but self-confidence, maturity, and a sense of direction, as well as network contacts (see Chapter 7). Many career actors in our sample actively pursued learning, both to become better at their jobs and as an investment in their own careers. Few were concerned that the learning developed in a company setting should necessarily be expended in that setting. In that respect, Damien's initial loyalty to his early "home" hotel, to which he kept returning, is unusual.

Most career actors accept that much crossing of inter-company boundaries and inter-industry boundaries is necessary if they are to maintain their learning momentum. Often the boundary-crossing occurs in people's pursuit of new learning. This has important implications for the many companies which seek to manage their human resources strategically by creating a corps of loyal company members pursuing success through ongoing advancement along company career paths. It also provides clues, we believe, to what is commonly called "organizational learning." As Damien moved between his first hotel and other restaurants, not only did he learn from all of these establishments, but they learned from each other through Damien's utilization and transmission of their special expertise. Careers, enacted over time, provide a mechanism for the ongoing transformation of the companies among whom career actors move (see Chapter 8).

Agency and Communion

Marshall draws on concepts of "agency" and "communion" to provide a sensemaking framework for understanding career behavior.[14] Agency and communion are contrasting forms of characteristic human responses to the uncertainties of life. Agency expresses independence through self-assertion and control over the environment. Communion expresses interdependence through openness and integration of oneself with the environment. Agency asserts itself in focused, direct action to alter or control the environment, while communion accepts the environment and its changes and adapts to it. Simply stated, agency is linked with doing and communion with being. An important difference between agentic and communal behaviors is in the response to others: employers, co-workers, family. Agency builds formal processes which enhance control. Communion evolves through relationships in a search for shared meaning.

As Marshall implies, traditional theories and conceptualizations of career are inherently sexist. The theories tended to assume male career stereotypes and to use male research samples.[15] They accepted agentic masculine career behavior as normative. For example, it was assumed that for the whole of a working life, from apprenticeship to retirement, work would be full-time, uninterrupted by childbearing or family considerations. Appreciation of career-relevant skills was confined to those acquired in conventional paid employment. Women's abilities and experience gained at home and in volunteer activities were devalued. Linear, bureaucratic, and hierarchical concepts of career epitomized by such phrases as "career planning," "career ladder," and "get to the top" were accepted as given and immutable.

Marshall suggests that the previous advocacy of "agency mitigated by communion" be modified to revalue women's experience through paths of "communion enhanced by agency."[16] Lives dominated by communion show a valuing of being rather than doing; connection through relationships over autonomy; cyclic rather than sequential patterns; whole lives rather than part lives; process-based development rather than an emphasis on goals and outcomes.

So far in this chapter, to highlight the opportunities for choosing and doing that the enactment perspective entails, we have emphasized the agentic component of careers. However, Gus not only acted agentically to reinvigorate his career, he also acted through relationships with old friends, and used his agentic success to enhance his family and community life. Priscilla and Gina were both agentic in developing their careers but also insisted that home life play a greater role in the future. Susan placed increasing importance on a sense of community and recreation with her peers in marketing.

Other cases in our sample, the majority women, offered evidence of a spirit of "communion enhanced by agency":

Communion first

Marie is a homemaker and schoolteacher. She is strongly identified with her profession but her deeper philosophy concerns being child-oriented and open to others. She somewhat wistfully dreams of spending more time on herself, but this is unlikely when reflected against years dedicated to the needs of children and the local community. Marie raised her own children before re-entering paid work at a school close to home. She is well networked and well regarded in her local community, and somewhat wryly comments, "I should be a social worker." However, she enjoys her work with the new entrants to junior school who come from a variety of ethnic groups. She values the love she receives from them and comments "we are like a little family." She nurtures their desire for learning by providing opportunities to motivate, to explore, and to discover. She also values what she gets from her colleagues, "support, professional ideology, camaraderie, and feeling that we are for a common goal." Marie's career story is that of communion first, not as a mindless dedication to others, but intertwined with a critical awareness of the limitations of government education policies and of changing social conditions.

Deferred communion

Dan had a very successful agentic career as a merchant banker, and was able to attain economic independence and semi-retire because of his financial investments. The job was a "young man's game," 12 hours a day plus, with demanding overseas travel. The decision to change was driven by the need for a different life style. "I've had a broken marriage, probably because I was working too hard." He is now married again and has a young daughter with whom he is able to spend time. He enjoys seeing more of all his children. Dan learned from the imbalance of his earlier experience, and concedes that he was fortunate to be able to do something about it. He has been able to have a second chance, to shift the balance to communion *enhanced* by agency. He is very happy, comfortable, and learning to be a "hands off operator" in his businesses, learning how to live more fully. Dan has not always been so guided by communion. However, he recognized the dis-ease of a life focused on a goal-centered work and the concomitant sacrifices that he had made to his personal relationships.

Many of the women members of our sample, even those who had a strong agentic commitment to their career, were touched and enlivened by their philosophy of communion and the focus on family and volunteer involvement which grew out of it. For these women, there was no "last boundary"[17] between work and home. Communion was an integral part of their being: their "careers" made no sense without reference to interconnections of life beyond paid work. In contrast, for many of the men, home was conceptualized as a backdrop to their career. Those few men for whom communion played a greater role were exceptions. Moreover, the exceptional behavior was often triggered by circumstances such as the attainment of economic success, the experience of disability, or losing a job. These circumstances extended time spent at home, as did affiliation with ethnic groups where communal life and extended family responsibilities were held in greater esteem.

A Framework

Looking back on this chapter, we can reflect on the broader set of themes around which the enactment of careers takes place. The early stories of Gus, the stevedore turned company owner, Priscilla, the trainee designer turned office manager, Gina, the factory worker turned day care center owner, all highlight the process through which the enactment of careers unfolds. The stories also show how career scripts develop and make retrospective sense across time. As time unfolds, the enactment process brings in interconnected themes concerning improvisation, adaptation, learning, sensemaking, and the balance between agency and communion. They also touch on themes of connectedness with the wider economic and social arenas in which careers occur, and on themes involving reciprocities and the strengthening and weakening of employment situations (see Chapter 1). The stories, and the contexts in which they have been told, are intended as a primer for the rest of this book. The themes we have outlined will be our companions throughout the chapters ahead.

First, however, we need a broad framework against which to arrange our basic data. For this purpose, we will use age-based career stage theory, but modify it to take account of the changing circumstances of the New Economy.

The essence of career theory is understanding sequences of behavior that take place over long periods of time. As indicated in Chapter 1, a traditional approach has been that of discerning, through observation, the "career stages" that individuals characteristically go through. There is some convergence in this area, revolving around popularized themes of "exploration" in the early career years, "advancement" in the middle years, and "maintenance" in the later years.[18] Affirmation of the three-stage view may be drawn from the broader life-stage models originally developed largely on male populations.[19] But theories such as these reflect the times in which they were created. Stable hierarchical structures populated by upwardly-mobile men create stable hierarchical career paths suitable for those who have no need to interrupt their careers for family reasons.

Traditional career theories do not reflect most women's experience. Women bring different dreams into adulthood, and, in contrast to the developmental sequence described for men, are likely to place affiliation and generativity ahead of advancement. Women (and now sometimes men) are also likely to take time off paid work in a way that interferes with the assumptions of traditional career pathing. Nevertheless, with some adjustment for underlying personal goals and priorities, a three-stage career model can still be discerned.[20]

A further complication is that as hierarchies are destabilized and restructured, and as occupational or industry learning and improvisation replace company-specific competencies, it becomes necessary to refine and revise theories of career development. Age-bound stereotypes – "new kid on the block," "fast-track," "new breed," "climbing the ladder," "at home looking after babies," "career woman," "faithful company servant," "time server," – become increasingly irrelevant. Individuals pursue "protean" careers[21] – changing career shapes and re-emphasizing different social roles continuously to take advantage of opportunities (or to forestall threats) in the new boundaryless environment. The developmental cycles of the work career become more and more involved, particularly for women, with those of home and family. Family stages and projects become interdependent with those of the career.[22] These changes sweep the three career stages into seamless stories of unique experience. At least, some changes do. Other changes remain mired in the assumptions of the past: permanent employment, hierarchical male careers, female casualization, occupational specialization without change, and of course development until retirement through the orderly stages of exploration, advancement, and maintenance.

Various writers, including some of the originators of career stage theory, now acknowledge the possibility of recycling through the major stages to accommodate changing personal circumstances.[23] A laid-off worker without marketable skills would have to enter the exploration stage again. So too would a long-term homemaker seeking to re-engage with the world of work. Other writers support these interpretations, as well as predicting their greater frequency in a more dynamic and uncertain employment arena. For example, Nicholson's theory of job transitions[24] includes phases of engagement with a new job which may be described as "preparation/encounter," "adjustment," and "stabilization." Mirvis and Hall[25] discuss "periodic plateauing" and renewed learning stages for workers in fields with short product- or technology-cycles. Boyatzis and Kolb[26] conceptualize recurrent interplay through three modes of individual adaptation and growth: "the *learning* mode as the quest for novelty; the *performance* mode as the quest for mastery; and the *development* mode as the quest for meaning." Weick[27] observes similarly, "In a boundaryless world, [the] development sequence continues to unfold, but it does so more quickly, with more intensity, in smaller gatherings. A lifetime of development is compressed into the lifetime of the project." (p. 50).

Applying the Framework

The challenge is to provide a picture of both the described "macro" (age-linked) and the "micro" (job- or project-linked) career cycles. We will do so by offering three chapters that accommodate the macro viewpoint while allowing disconformity from it. Most of our examples will reflect the tidy age-linked agenda that traditional career theory suggests. However, some will clearly be exceptions to normative career stage assumptions. Also, most of our examples will also reflect more "micro" cycles in which people engage, albeit within longer encompassing career trajectories. All of our examples illustrate the enactment process – of people making sense of their careers as they go, and using that sensemaking to guide their further career agendas.

In Chapter 4, "Fresh Energy," we consider behaviors that are driven by the desire for exploration and novelty. We look at "career entry" activities. We see how new jobs, projects, and directions can energize the career and provide fresh learning. We also consider the major role that chance, or happenstance, plays in "altering the ground" in people's careers, creating novelty even though there has been no particular quest for it. We find that few careers stand as logical constructs created by wise career actors planning progressive mastery through stable, sympathetic institutions. Most involve a stage or stages emphasizing the enactment of novelty, experiment, and creative responses to unpredictable situations.

In Chapter 5 we consider "Informed Direction," the process which most people understand to be at the heart of career planning and action. In informed direction, career actors establish momentum and direction through projects, jobs, and careers. As they do so, they frequently find that direction is facilitated or constrained by aspects of wider social roles, such as marriage partnerships and family responsibilities. They inform themselves about options and constraints, make choices and investments – for example, in occupations or in employers – as they seek to advance towards their goals. We look at the dangers as well as the advantages of directed career behavior as the institutions in which career actors make their investments respond over time.

In Chapter 6, "Seasoned Engagement," we consider job and career behavior in the mature stages of careers, or of cycles within those careers. Traditionally, people are expected to capitalize on their previous career investments. However, some seek to capitalize before the associated career stage. Others may find their skills have lost much of their value, and experience boredom or layoff. But for many career actors, the challenge is to adapt to their own changing social roles, interests, and energy. They need to remain flexible in a still-changing world. Adaptation may be gentle and gradual, or cataclysmic and sudden, but as the actor's life circumstances change it is always cumulative. Older career actors often have to "hold on" in their work roles until retirement, or else take conscious steps to revitalize their careers by stepping back into "fresh energy" mode.

We will turn in Chapter 7 to focus more explicitly on the "micro" cycles within people's careers, and the contribution those cycles make to larger institutional and economic activities.

Notes

1. Weick, K.E. *Sensemaking in Organizations*. Thousand Oaks, CA: Sage Publications, 1995; Weick, K.E., Enactment and the boundaryless career: organizing as we work. In M.B. Arthur and D.M. Rousseau (eds.) *The Boundaryless Career*. New York: Oxford University Press, 1996, pp. 40–57.

2. Mischel, W. The interaction of person and situation. In D. Magnuson and N.S. Endler (eds.) *Personality at the Crossroads*. Hillsdale, NJ: Erlbaum, 1977.

3. Hughes, E.C. *Men and Their Work*. Glencoe, IL: Free Press, 1958, p. 67.

4. Barley, S.R. Careers, identities and institutions: the legacy of the Chicago School of Sociology. In M.B. Arthur, D.T. Hall and B.S. Lawrence (eds.) *Handbook of Career Theory*. New York: Cambridge University Press, 1989, pp. 44–65.

5. Weick, K.E. *The Social Psychology of Organizing* (2nd ed.). Reading, MA: Addison-Wesley, 1979.

6. This section draws from Gioia, T. *The Imperfect Art*. New York: Oxford University Press, 1988.

7. Mintzberg, H. Crafting strategy. *Harvard Business Review*, 1987, July/August, pp. 66–75.

8. Gioia, op. cit. (6), p. 61.

9. Weick, 1995, op. cit. (1).

10. Weick, 1996, op. cit. (1), p. 40.

11. Bateson, M.C. *Peripheral Visions: Learning Along the Way*. New York: Harper Collins, 1994.

12. Argyris, C. and Schön, D. *Organizational Learning: A Theory of Action Perspective*. Reading, MA: Addison-Wesley, 1978.

13. Bird, A. Careers as repositories of knowledge: considerations for boundaryless careers. In Arthur and Rousseau, op. cit. (1), pp. 150–68.

14. Marshall, J. Re-visioning career concepts: a feminist invitation. In Arthur, Hall and Lawrence, op. cit. (4). Also see Bakan, D. *The Duality of Human Existence*. Boston: Beacon, 1966.

15. For example, Levinson, D.J., Darrow, C.N., Levinson, M.H. and McKee, B. *The Seasons of a Man's Life*. New York: Knopf, 1978; Schein, E.H. *Career Dynamics: Matching Individual and Organizational Needs*. Reading, MA: Addison-Wesley, 1978.

16. Marshall, J. In Arthur, Hall and Lawrence, op. cit. (4).

17. Fletcher, J.K. and Bailyn, L. Challenging the last boundary: reconnecting work and family. In Arthur and Rousseau, op. cit. (1), pp. 256–67.

18. Super, D.E. *The Psychology of Careers*. New York: Harper & Row, 1957.

19. Erikson, E.H. Identity and the life cycle. *Psychological Issues*, 1957, 1 (1): 1–177; and Levinson et al., op. cit. (15).

20. Gilligan, C. *In a Different Voice: Psychological Theory and Women's Development*. Cambridge, MA: Harvard University Press, 1982; Levinson, D.J., Darrow, C.N., Klein, E.B., Levinson, M.H. and McKee, B. *The Seasons of a Woman's Life*. New York: Knopf, 1996.

21. Hall, D.T. *Careers in Organizations*. Pacific Palisades, CA: Goodyear, 1976.

22. Sekeran, U. and Hall, D.T. Asynchronism in dual-career and family linkages. In Arthur, Hall and Lawrence, op. cit. (4), pp. 159–80.

23. Arthur, M.B. and Kram, K.E. Reciprocities at work: the separate, yet inseperable, possibilities for individual and organizational development. In Arthur, Hall, and Lawrence, op. cit. (4), pp. 292–312; Super, D.E. (1990). A life-span, life-space approach to career development. In D. Brown and L. Brooks (eds.) *Career Choice and Development*, San Francisco: Jossey-Bass, 1990.

24. Nicholson, N. A theory of work role transitions. *Administrative Science Quarterly*, 1984, 29: 172–91.

25. Mirvis, P.H. and Hall, D.T. Psychological success and the boundaryless career. In Arthur and Rousseau, op. cit., pp. 237–255.

26. Boyatzis, R.E. and Kolb, D.A. Performance, learning, and development as modes of growth and adaptation throughout our lives and careers. In M.A. Peiperl, M.B. Arthur, R. Goffee and T. Morris (eds) *Career Frontiers: New Conceptions of Working Life*, Oxford: Oxford University Press, in press.

27. Sekeran and Hall, op. cit. (22); Weick, 1996, op. cit. (1).

4 Fresh Energy: Engaging with Unfamiliar Situations

Finding One's Self

Wendy would have liked to do art and languages at school, but was forced by her parents to take clerical subjects. She left at 17 and took an office junior position, but found clerical work boring. She moved away from home and enrolled at university for a course in applied design. But she found the relative poverty of student life difficult, and became homesick. She decided to return home and rejoin the workforce. Through a contact of her mother's she obtained a job in the office of a transportation company, but again, "I was unmotivated by it . . . I hated it, it was really boring." She stayed 18 months.

Wendy next obtained a customer service job with a broadcasting company. The company rotated Wendy to other departments, and as well as learning telephone customer service she dabbled in quality assurance, internal promotions, and sales administration. She began to see the range of possibilities in a company setting: "I like to think it's where my career started."

After two years she went overseas for a "working vacation," supporting herself with the work she could find along the way. "That's where my life changed . . . I became really focused and I had more direction . . . it gave me a lot of self-confidence, you have to really sell yourself." She secured a job as sales administrator in a small distribution company, co-ordinating orders, selling, delivering, cold calling. Her previous jobs had given her relevant accounting experience, technical knowledge and customer service training. She was poorly paid, but enjoyed the variety and responsibility of the job. After a trip home with a new partner, and some further customer service work, she secured residency in her partner's country and returned there with him. She found a sales administration job with a pharmaceutical company, a good job with her own client base. But her relationship broke up and once more she returned to her home country.

Wendy decided to rejoin the broadcasting company to try to build up a good employment record there. But before she could start, she saw a newspaper ad for a job as a marketing assistant in the pharmaceutical industry: "The description of the person they were looking for really sounded like me, so I went after the job . . . it was meant to be, there was some divine intervention . . . the reason why I got that other job in the [overseas] pharmaceutical company was to try and prepare me for this job."

She feels that at last she has found herself, in an industry and a job where she can be happy. "I intend to stay as long as I can . . . I took this job on thinking that I want to spend the next five years here, between two and five years, I wouldn't leave before two years, but . . . I think I might get a bit bored. I definitely want to stay in the pharmaceutical industry if I can."

Wendy's first ten years in the workforce were characterized by exploration and experimentation. She did not set goals and work towards them. She did not make a career choice, such as "I want to be a designer," or "I want to be in marketing" and execute a pre-determined plan. Rather, she explored, trying different jobs until she found something that fitted, for the time being at least.

Wendy's mode of finding her way in the world would be instantly recognizable to many career theorists, particularly those who have charted age-related stages or phases of career development. Such theories typically characterize early career as a time of finding one's way, either in life in general, or in a specific employment situation. In keeping with Donald Super, several writers see a stage of "exploration" from adolescence until the late twenties or early thirties.[1] In this stage, the career actor goes through a process of "reality testing" as he or she explores the environment and tries to relate aspects of self-identity to it so as to retain those aspects that bring satisfaction. The essential dynamic is not just of exploration but of experiment and trial-and-error refinement. Behaviorally, career actors in this mode often display intense passion, exuberance, and creativity.[2] It is this vitality, and the patterns of motivation and behavior associated with it, that causes "Fresh Energy."

Exploration, says Super, is not necessarily conscious or systematic, but open and tentative, and needs to be so:

> Sometimes exploration is so highly focused that it precludes consideration of alternatives, as when a son or daughter pursues from early childhood an occupational objective inspired or set by a parent or other adult. Such early foreclosure sometimes leads to later dissatisfaction.[3]

The problem of early foreclosure is emphasized by what Levinson and his colleagues see as a normative "Age Thirty Transition," a roughly five-year period "to work on the flaws and limitations of the preceding adult years."[4]

However, even unsystematic experimental career behavior is seldom random. It is, as it were, inductive rather than deductive science. The experiments are exercises in cumulative adaptation, informed by learning and often by a wish to break out of the confines of current jobs and try new ways of self-expression. The rewards become evident in the long-term, when the accumulated outcomes of short-term choices become life stories, to be observed retrospectively and interpreted. Career actors may be unconsciously wiser about their own dispositions, their own learning, and their own long-term needs, than are their educational institutions, vocational advisors, and companies. They will find direction when they need to.

Thus, Wendy experienced disappointment when she followed adult-assisted early attempts to find direction through vocational training and clerical work. By moving autonomously and experimentally, she began to "find herself" and build a worthwhile and focused career, though even by age 28 it was clear that exploration was probably not over for her. If we review the careers of the younger members of our sample, her pattern is typical.

Some might regret the apparent inefficiency of these patterns, the loss of ongoing productive focus as career actors cast about to find interest or identity. After all, the goal of much education and training, and particularly career counselling work, is to help people to get on track in their careers more quickly. We take a different view. Every experience is an opportunity for learning. The wider the range of experiences, the wider the range of skills available to be acquired. To make sense of the past, and to find direction for the future, we need a variety of career experiences.

Lastly, we want to dispel any notion that novelty-seeking, exploration and experimentation in career behavior is necessarily confined to the early career years. While age/stage theories are a means of helping us to see common patterns over the whole course of a person's working life, no theorist would claim that the stages have rigid age-defined boundaries. Super and others have now recognized that any career actor, at any age, might "cycle through" novelty and other motives in relation to a particular job, or even a short-term project.[5] Boyatzis and Kolb identify a "learning mode" of career behavior which can occur or recur at any stage of the career; it is characterized by a preoccupation with "novelty, variety, and generalizability."[6] We may see phases of "fresh energy" at any stage of any adult's career, as older career actors interrupt established tracks and revisit the restless wandering and zigzag energy of their youth. Some make major career shifts relatively late in life, which are often driven by the desire for novelty or major change.[7] Others pursue novelty constantly within the safe confines of a single job, by reorganizing what they do and taking new initiatives. The oldest participant in our study became a square-dancer at 65, following a career of manual labor.

Notionally, therefore, this chapter is about career exploration by any career actor. In fact, however, the chapter will focus largely on younger people. Not only did they tend to demonstrate "fresh energy" more frequently and more vividly than did other groups, they also faced common issues which are undoubtedly age-related: breaking away from parents and home, establishing work identity, thinking about and often finding a partner, perhaps starting a family.

The detail of Wendy's story embodies many mechanisms and experiences common in our sample for younger actors in the early years of their careers. Thus, she experienced:

- discontinuities in her early career as she experimented and sought to find her way in the world;
- periods of "getting away" in which learning was accelerated in new settings;
- a "self-designed apprenticeship" as she found her own learning agenda, and traded immediate earnings for learning of long-term value;
- defining moments of insight as she made retrospective sense of discontinuous and exploratory early career experience and established broad plans for the future.

While this form of restless enactment is especially true for career beginners, we see it also among older career actors, as they interrupt established tracks and reconnect with the exploration more typical of early career behavior. They lose enthusiasm for established career tracks or current jobs and projects, and channel their energies in new directions:

- resolving career dissatisfaction by moving suddenly into an unrelated activity;
- using a period of maternity leave or child-rearing as a period of reflection and self-evaluation before revitalising one's career in a new field;
- developing novel projects to enliven work.

In this chapter we look at the surges of experimental, exploratory, curiosity-driven behavior that provide careers with their essential exuberance.

Virtue in Discontinuity

Students in higher education often have a linear view of the correspondence between their current training and their future careers.
They inquire earnestly into the career potential of courses in operations management or marketing. They tend to believe that all engineering students spend their lives as engineers, and all education
students spend their lives as teachers. Yet experience suggests that in
the transition between higher educational experiences and early
career development, disjunction is common.

In many lives, career stories appear to be discontinuous. There are
sudden shifts and zigzag moves as individuals pursue novelty,
conduct temporary experiments, and shift around, seeking direction
for their lives.

A Zigzag Career

Brett after leaving school without distinguishing himself, spent a year in
Europe, where he had a girl friend. At that stage he wanted to go into
farming. But "I didn't want to work for someone else for 20 years being a
farm manager . . . I'd rather get rich first and buy a farm. So I went to
university and did business." Brett paid his way by means of temporary and
vacation jobs. But at the university he "didn't work very hard, drank a lot of
beers, and only had half a degree after three years." Brett quit the
university, walked down to the factory at the end of his road and got a job.
He learned to drive a forklift, do four-wheel skids, even to smoke marijuana.
He also played in a band. But after six months he got bored with the
factory, walked out, and went on unemployment benefits for six months.

But Brett's parents were "hassling me to get a decent job." One morning,
he "got up, cut my hair, went out and bought a suit and walked around a
few stock exchange places, and got a job." The Exchange was in a bull
phase, and "what they wanted was a smart cookie, basically." Initially Brett
had a clerical job. He "saved my boss a lot of money" by negotiating with
clients over the phone - "I did really well at that" - and the firm decided to
give him a chance on the trading floor. He spent three months just
observing, then became an operator. "That was really good, down on the
floor with a lot of people yelling and screaming, buying and selling shares.
It's a sort of cowboy's [environment], a lot of bravado and stuff. If you're a
good bargainer and you've got quite a strong personality you'll do well."

For Brett, the stock exchange job was an experiment. "I just wanted to
know that I could do it." But, successful as Brett was from an objective
viewpoint, subjectively his career change was not working for him. "I got a
picture of the world, what it is like in the business world, suit world, paper
world in the inner city. And basically I realized it wasn't me. All the people
there were dorks, most of them. All they wanted was a Porsche and a

blonde girlfriend, and to be [more hip] than the next guy." Still interested in entertainment, Brett used to "turn up on a uni-cycle to work, and go street performing outside the stock exchange in my suit . . . to the chagrin of my boss . . . I got my briefcase to collect the coins. Singing songs about the end of the world."

Eventually the stock exchange experienced a major market crash. Soon afterwards a colleague of Brett's embezzled a large sum of money. Stung by his boss's accusation that he should have known, Brett walked out. "A lot of people were getting laid off with [some] pay. I didn't get that, I just walked."

Brett quickly obtained a temporary casual job painting a boat for a boat-builder. The boat-builder turned out also to be a plasterer, and on completion of the boat job, "he said, 'Come plastering with me'. So the next four days after that I spent on a job, plastering with him. And after about four days I thought, 'This is a lark, I'll go and do it myself.'" To the disappointment of the plasterer, who "knew I was good, and thought he could use me," Brett walked out to seek plastering jobs on his own. A plastering apprenticeship normally takes four years. But "I'm really good with my hands. I spent a lot of time when I was young carving and sculpturing, building stuff out of plaster. I got it from my Dad." Also, "I taught myself most of the plastering out of a book I got in the library. It was an old English Guild book, that's where I got the ornamental stuff from. I don't think they teach it at technical college."

And so, for the past seven years, Brett has made his main income as a self-employed plasterer. He does "a lot of ornamental stuff . . . ceiling restorations and facades of old concrete buildings." He has built a reputation: he never advertises, clients call him. He employs his unemployed friends as helpers. "Socially it's a really good job, working with people you like. And you can get about. It's flexible, I can stop for a few months, go on [vacation]."

In addition, Brett has continued with the entertainment interests he showed in his earlier work as a band member and street performer. One day he went along to a theatrical agent who sent him for an audition for a popular local television "soap". He got the part, which led to parts in a number of other programs and films. Nowadays he spends perhaps a month a year in acting work. He also does radio work, and plays the guitar in a band two nights a week.

Since he became a plasterer, Brett has thought of moving twice. On one occasion he became involved with a woman whose career was overseas, a near-recycling of his early experience of Europe. But in the end they decided not to go ahead. He has also seriously considered trying to go into music on a full-time basis, but gave up the idea because of the potential insecurity. "When you've got no money at all you're completely disempowered. I like driving a car, good food, and living in a nice house."

Looking back on his career, Brett thinks he has become a "jack of all trades." He would like to "become master of one, focus on one area." He thinks he may "work as a plasterer for a couple [more] years . . . make enough money to buy some long-term assets, then, start developing the acting and music side, full-time."

Brett is creative, and trips lightly through his career, enacting work, recreation, and interaction with friends to give himself the lifestyle he wants. His learning has been driven by his current self-determined needs. It has been anarchic, and he has apparently gained more value towards his current career from a book that he found in his local library than from his formal education at a respectable university. Now, his skill and reputation protect his security and lifestyle. He enjoys the fulfillment he gets from his ability to do quality work, and the recognition he receives from clients. He indulges his creative interests on a part-time basis. His self-employed status gives him the autonomy he wants.

Brett's career is currently in a relatively continuous phase, albeit with some variety and discontinuity within it as he periodically embarks on new projects. Previously it contained some startling discontinuities. The past seven years have been based on a sudden switch from professional/commercial work to trade/manual work, and have turned on a chance encounter with a plastering specialist when Brett was seeking casual employment. This seems a tenuous base from which to build a career. Some might consider that Brett has wasted the time he spent at the university – he eventually completed his degree on a part-time basis – and doing stock exchange work. But although he did not follow up his earlier career opportunities, they were important in providing him with insight into his own tastes and ambitions, and some elementary social and business skills. Viewing his career in retrospect, Brett can make good sense of it.

Like Brett, few of the other young people in our sample had sustained the direction in which their initial choices pointed. Among twelve young career actors aged under 40 who had pursued higher education or trade qualifications directly from school or soon afterwards, only three were still working in a job directly related to their training (Table 4.1). Several discovered from practical experience that what may have seemed like a good idea in the abstract arena of discussions with parents or school careers advisors, simply was not, in practice, what they felt comfortable with. This is not to say that the time spent in pursuing these qualifications was necessarily wasted. Most appeared to have valued the experiences as opportunities for generalizable learning, and increased self-confidence and self-understanding. Knowledge of one's own disinclinations can be valuable.

Among young career actors who left school without pursuing further qualifications, similar patterns of drift and experiment were apparent. In most cases the teens and early twenties appeared to be too soon for the career actors to establish direction. This is not to say that initial choices left no legacy. In some cases (including Wendy's)

Table 4.1 *Initial pursuit of qualifications vs job at time of interview*

Name	Initial qualification	Job at time of interview
Albert	Civil engineering diploma	Technical sales/bar manager
Brett	Commerce degree	Plasterer
Catherine	Accounting degree	Marketing manager
Damien	*Auto glazing apprenticeship	Chef
Glenda	Optometry degree	Optometrist
Jack	Welding apprenticeship	Health care worker
Julie	*Arts degree	Union organizer
Kirsty	Arts degree	Retailer
Martin	Certificate in mechanical engineering	Own engineering business
Owen	*Accounting – professional studies	Oyster farmer
Susan	Food technology degree	Product manager (non-food)
Wendy	*Applied design degree	Marketing assistant

* Program of studies not completed.

these jobs focused a clear sense of the type of career to be avoided. In others they led indirectly to new opportunities that were more attractive than the initial choices made.

Unexpected outcomes from early jobs

Barry's first job in a supermarket taught him an important lesson about himself: he didn't like working in a "people" setting where he had to deal with the public. He got a warehouse job where he "didn't have to be nice to everyone," and has been in relatively solitary jobs ever since.

Julie worked regularly in a fast-food outlet to help pay her way through university. Her family had been involved in trade union activity, and she had empathy with working people. Her co-workers elected her as their union representative and later she accepted the union's invitation to take a full-time organizer's position.

Sally's first job and second job were as a secretary-receptionist in advertising agencies. These led to her becoming a media planner, the starting-point of a growing reputation and a successful career in advertising.

Going Away and Getting Smarter

Many career actors had undertaken periods of travel, working vacations where they made a living from jobs away from home. Wendy's early career, for example, included a year away at a distant university and two periods of self-sponsored overseas experience.

Overseas experience provides rich opportunities for novel cultural experience. It is one way of satisfying the urge that many young people feel, to get away from the familiar – the family, the job, the neighborhood, the predictable routines – and to see, and often do, something different. Over half of the younger members of our sample and many of the older ones had travelled overseas. Although overseas travel tends to be a middle-class activity, we found variants on the going away theme among other workers who had simply gone to the city, or changed cities, in their own search for fresh experience.

The young travellers had invariably acted proactively as executors of their own development. They saved their money, applied for work permits, resigned from their local jobs, took off to faraway places, and looked for casual employment. Their travel was not conventional career development: destinations were selected mainly for interest rather than work opportunities. Work was chosen less to enhance careers in a direct, skill-building way, but more to put money in their pockets and to keep them mobile. Thus, a computer programmer might spend a few weeks as a waiter in a foreign café rather than working at his personal computer, and might acquire interpersonal skills, self-confidence, and foreign languages rather than computer languages. Elsewhere, we have argued that such experiences have a hidden value, because they assist the development of flexibility, multiple skills, self-confidence, and enterprise – exactly the characteristics most necessary for economic survival and prosperity in the New Economy.[8]

In these circumstances especially, the learning that has taken place becomes evident only in retrospect, as former travellers enact the fragments of apparently formless careers into powerful patterns of self-directed enterprise or cope-with-anything versatility. As we have seen, Wendy found that being independent in a strange country forced her to develop self-confidence and gave her a new sense of direction. She was not alone.

Career Development through Travel

Bruce (Chapter 3) used overseas work experience in the hotel trade to add service and managerial skills to a technical base and transform himself from an itinerant boilermaker to a respectable sales professional.

Joan left a dead-end laboratory assistant job to go overseas in her mid-20s. She travelled for two and a half years, supporting herself through casual work. When she returned she transformed her travel experience into a virtue by earning a place on a travel agency training program, and building a new career.

Kirsty gained insight into retailing and customer service through working overseas in a flower shop. When she returned home, the self-confidence and retail skills she had acquired helped her in setting up a successful flooring business.

Phillip, a trained government town planner, travelled with his partner to "see the world." Near the end of his trip, he got a job in a private planning consultancy. On his return home he used the knowledge gained to set up his own business.

The Self-Designed Apprenticeship

In Wendy's early career, she explored new types of work, and built a competency base involving clerical, accounting, sales, customer service, distribution, administrative and marketing skills. Her "self-designed" apprenticeship had no definable learning objectives or target job. She literally made it up as she went along. Sometimes she sacrificed immediate rewards for the sake of autonomy and learning. Yet, when she saw her most recent job advertised, it seemed to her that her past had been a purpose-built preparation for it.

Wendy's experience contrasts with models of apprenticeship and vocational education, which seem increasingly preoccupied with specifying learning objectives, competencies, or other "outputs." Most members of our sample neither used this kind of terminology nor modeled such learning principles in their own development. They defined their goals broadly rather than narrowly, found their own opportunities to learn, conducted experiments, extended them if they seemed to work, pursued novel experience, selected their own instructors and mentors, and valued their learning in retrospect. It was they themselves rather than a profession gatekeeper or college bureaucrat who determined what learning was worthwhile. We call this the "self-designed apprenticeship."

Our data are full of examples. (Brett's brief practical self-introduction to plastering is one).

Self-Designed Apprenticeships

Albert, a newly graduated engineer, could find no professional jobs, so he got a bar job: "I said I'd work for free for a couple of weeks, just to see what it was like." He stayed for a year and learned the trade. A year after that, now established with a good engineering-based job, he returned to evening bar work and was soon promoted to night manager. Albert banks his night earnings, and is considering an opportunity to invest his savings to become part-owner of a bar.

Christine had a relative with Down's syndrome, and while at school did volunteer work for people with disabilities. Later in her clerical career she volunteered for work teaching children with disabilities, and devoted considerable leisure time to this. She learned sign language and assisted the deaf. Recently she has given up her job to train to be a teacher of people with disabilities.

Jeff, a draftsman, decided to become a gardener and landscape designer. Capitalizing on visualization skills developed in drafting, and an interest in gardening gained in his family, Jeff started to work as a gardener charging a low hourly rate. He chose interesting gardens to work in, and clients with expert knowledge. He also developed a friendship with an experienced landscape designer, a mentor who introduced him to some of his clients. Through his expertise and connections, Jeff has developed a highly successful business.

Damien worked for seven years as a trainee chef largely in a single hotel, to which he remained loyal. But "from time to time I would leave and go and get experience elsewhere . . . I wanted as much knowledge as I could." Other hotels had different styles of cuisine and service, and he would join specifically to learn the new skills. Within his "home" hotel he would volunteer for novel work. To learn managerial skills he watched the different leadership styles of the chefs he worked under. He went overseas and managed the kitchen of an English pub. He is now the head chef in a large restaurant.

While a number of these stories ended in self-employment, the self-designed apprenticeship also applies to employment settings. For example, in cases previously considered, Priscilla (Chapter 3) engineered a well-rounded apprenticeship in the design industry from within the confines of her employing organization; Catherine (Chapter 2) devised her self-designed apprenticeship in marketing by utilizing a college and a telecommunications company. Both were mobile, seeking new experiences after they had mastered each new role.

For those seeking to upgrade skills, or to make a fresh start, the self-designed apprenticeship has considerable advantages over the formal one. Because there is no predetermined end-point, it is adaptable to the apprentice's changing self-insights and skills. Because the curriculum is based not on the abstract design of an expert but on the evolving curiosity of the apprentice, boredom and irrelevance are unlikely. Because there are no formal ties to employers or training institutions, the self-designed apprenticeship can cross inter-job, inter-company, and even international boundaries relatively easily.

The self-designed apprenticeship also overcomes a frequent problem of formal apprenticeship: the signaling to the apprentice that apprenticeship is "time served" and that the qualification lasts for the rest of his or her life. Far more than the conventional apprenticeship, the self-designed apprenticeship enables the apprentice to develop habits of curiosity and cumulative learning which can be extended throughout the career.

Moments of Truth

Cumulative adaptation (Chapter 3) is often punctuated by energizing "moments of truth," when the career turns on an insight or revelation that provides a powerful interpretation of the person's past, present, and future. Wendy experienced such a moment when she saw a newspaper advertisement for a pharmaceutical job, and realized that her previous career experiences had been guiding her towards that job in that industry. In other cases sensemaking may be more gradual, as the individual develops clarity or resolution incrementally over time. Such insights have a powerful effect in mobilizing the person's energy in a new direction.

Fishing for Direction

Owen had fled from a boring apprenticeship in accountancy before he was 20 to a period of adventure including working on a charter boat and in fairgrounds. Settling down somewhat, he completed a degree in biology. He was employed in government research, but soon discovered that "I had had enough of sitting inside in a laboratory," so he spent a year working on his parents' farm. He next found a short-term job as a scientific observer on deep-sea fishing boats.

But a girlfriend went overseas and Owen followed her. He worked for a commercial mariner, painting, sailing, and exhibiting boats. Then he and his girlfriend went travelling, ending up six months later in England. He was beginning to develop an interest in aquaculture. He landed a job in trout farming and developed some experience in the breeding and rearing of fish. After ten months, with itchy feet once more, he and his girlfriend took off around Europe in a van. At an aquaculture conference Owen had met the owner of a scallop farm in Scotland who needed farmhands. On their return from the continent Owen and his girlfriend took up the owner's offer. And at that point, Owen realized what he wanted:

"I wanted to work with another life form as opposed to that more complicated like trout. I wanted to work where the environment was the controlling factor, rather than the human. The oyster farmers and scallop farmers rely entirely on the food that comes from the ocean." His mind clear, and wanting to be with family and friends, Owen went home.

He had little trouble getting short-term contracts in fisheries research. It enabled him to access aquaculture information. He bought an oyster-farming lease and began to develop it in his free time. Currently he has three jobs: June to January, oyster farming; January to May tree pruning; and ongoing contract work writing computer programs. He looks forward to "doing oyster farming for the rest of my life."

Owen's career combines different modes of career development: carefree adventure and travel; emergent direction as his interests gradually focus down to zoology, to fisheries work, to fish farming, to mollusks, and finally to oysters; proactive learning, as he accumulates technical competencies, self-reliance, and interpersonal skills; and the "moment of truth" in Scotland, as he makes sense of and integrates the strands of his past, to find a clear long-term mission for his future. There are many other examples.

Moments about New Industries

Desmond had a successful early career in administration in the transportation industry. By the age of 22 he had a management position, but was working long hours and experiencing high stress. In a "moment of truth" he realized that this was not the life for him, resigned his job and took a 3-month "time out" laboring position in an uncle's vineyard. This move led to his developing a career in the wine industry, but one which capitalizes on the administrative skills developed earlier.

Elaine was a mailroom supervisor. One day she saw a television program based on the law courts and felt attracted to the idea of being a court clerk. She phoned the local court and secured a job, even though it involved a salary cut. Twenty years on, she has developed her career to become a deputy court registrar.

Maternity as Transition

A special type of novelty-seeking behavior apparently took place during the pregnancies of women career actors. In discussing the effects of childbirth on their careers, very few of the women indicated that they had taken maternity leave and then returned to the same workplace. Instead, for those women who had made a heavy commitment to paid work for years, having a baby often presented an opportunity for reflection and a new direction. In all the cases in our study that shift was from an agentic engagement with their lives to one emphasizing communion and connection. Change was gradual, as women took time to reflect on their lives and redirect them.

Novelty through Pregnancy

Isabel pursued an academic scientific research career for more than a decade, but recently took maternity leave to care for her second child. She has an open invitation to return to her employer but has so far declined. She felt fulfilled in her paid work, and enjoyed a supportive working environment. However, she is now in a transition period, and the leave has given her time for reassessment. "I've always been torn, I felt my interests and skills were in different directions." Now Isabel is learning about children. Although she is unclear about her future direction it is unlikely that she will return to her past employment. Instead she would like to do something "that is of direct benefit to people."

Sally spent ten years in advertising, and is now on maternity leave. Having a baby was the catalyst for Sally to make a dramatic career shift. Previously, she was totally involved in work, "hungry to be challenged" and "working 80 hours a week." From her position on maternity leave she now sees things differently. "I still have my hand in, but I'm not really playing it. . . . There are other things in life besides a job, and I see lots of people I've worked with now, and young girls, and their career is really important to them. One thing I've learned. Don't give your all to it, because it really is unimportant." She looks back on her advertising career as a hectic hiatus in her life, one which she has now grown beyond. "It is the most useless occupation that there is." Sally has no plans for full-time work at present. She enjoys her domestic life, does some contract work, and has become conscious of issues in women's employment such as flexibility and the need to make the workplace more family friendly.

Catherine (Chapter 2) pursued a busy ten-year professional career, moving nearer and nearer to her goal of functional responsibility for a marketing department. But when she reached it, she found herself frustrated by her boss and by the stresses in the job. She became pregnant, so she left: "It was quite a handy excuse." She is considering part-time options, such as starting a business from home, and looks forward to a period of relative domesticity.

These examples demonstrate the value of reflection and apparent career passivity in giving Isabel, Sally, and Catherine a renewed sense of direction and purpose. Time out of paid work has regenerated their life work and brought them more into balance and a greater sense of wholeness. The women were all in their thirties, a common transitional period.[9] In this reflective time they questioned not only their previous roles but issues that arise for women in employment more generally.

Sally, like Dan (Chapter 3), demonstrates a radical shift from a fiercely agentic approach to life to one of communion. Reflective time away from agentic career activity does not sit well within conventional expectations of career progress. But the period is not seen as a plateau, or a dip, or even a pause, in the enactment of the career. Rather, in a boundaryless career environment actors "cycle" around varied arenas of life apparently without direction. However, internally the cumulative progress continues. In terms of learning and personal development, life changes may be incubating, as stories are shaped to turn along new paths.

Putting Bread on the Table

Many young workers, such as Wendy, are able to progress their careers through self-designed apprenticeships, experimentation, and learning. But there are others, typically those entering the workforce without credentials or skills, for whom the early years in a job or career are connected with more mundane matters. For them, work is less "career" than "job," and the function of "job" is to make a living. In the ongoing struggle to "put bread on the table," exploration and growth may be sacrificed.

From Job to Job to Job

Troy's background involved poverty and crime. He has brothers who have been in prison. He left school as soon as he could. Living at home with his parents, he felt a strong obligation to pay for his keep. His first job was in a chicken factory, where he showed enough perseverance to be promoted to supervisor. But after three years he was unfairly fired on suspicion of theft. By this time his girlfriend had had a baby, increasing his responsibilities. He found a laboring job in a metal foundry, but after four years the company relocated and he couldn't afford to go with them. He was next hired by a waste disposal owner/driver on a garbage collection round, emptying the bins. He enjoys the job and has a strong admiration for his boss. At 28, his aspirations are modest: to "be a family man," stay together with his girlfriend and son, and keep working. His boss has promised to let him drive the truck one day.

Troy's career does not "develop" in any conventional sense; rather, his jobs enable him to meet family responsibilities. As a manual worker, he is one of a dwindling breed. He has done little in his life that cannot be automated. With over 30 years of his career still to run, he seems a likely casualty in the knowledge society. Yet Troy has shown persistence and resilience. He has avoided unemployment, met his family obligations, and shown greater loyalty to successive employers than they have shown to him. People like Troy represent untapped labor-force potential.

Fortunately, there was evidence from elsewhere in our study that actors are able to make progress from basic "bread-on-the-table" work.

Finding a Way

Barry, a machine setter, has been stimulated by the combination of his routine work and a recognition of his long-term commitments to wife and family, He has enrolled for some night courses in engineering, and is increasingly identifying as an engineer rather than a laborer.

Lily followed her long-service aunt into a factory job "lifting sacks of powder, mixing them, and lifting boxes." After having two children she took a three-month course in clerical work, leading to an accounts clerk job, which she has been in for eight years, with steadily growing confidence.

Sargent had been stuck in elementary jobs until age 18. His father, alarmed at his lack of progress, sent an application on his behalf to the fire service, where he subsequently built his career as a firefighter.

Tommy, a farm laborer, realized through the illness of the farmer for whom he worked that he was better at running the farm than his boss. He applied for and obtained a farm management position.

Radical Transition

Discovering Identity Through Occupational Change

Jack left school in a provincial town and became an apprentice fitter and welder in a local company. He gained responsibility and developed his learning. After three years he earned his trade certification. He continued to work for the same company. But "the job was becoming repetitive." He obtained an advanced welding certificate and asked his boss if he could try for a higher-level engineering certificate. But the boss "didn't think it was worth going that far . . . after that I started to look elsewhere." He left his job, took a few months' vacation, and went to the city to live with relatives. His uncle helped him to get a job as a health assistant in a psychiatric clinic. His work involved supervising patients in their daily living and recreation, working in a team, and acquiring technical and legal knowledge. His ethnic background helped him to "relate to the cultural burdens that have stayed with clients" (from the same ethnic group). He also worked part-time in another clinic, and taught C.P.R.. He ran a sports team at work. Jack finds his job "fascinating. I know I can fall back into welding, but I've got into a job that's totally different. I didn't expect that, but I feel good about it." But once again, he is beginning to feel "blocked" – frustrated by the fact that there is no easy route from nurse aide to nurse. He also wants to return to his ethnic group to learn more about the culture. Further redirection in Jack's career is likely.

Radical career change typically arises from a deep-seated discontent or feeling of stagnation, and a desire to start afresh. The new start may be accompanied by revitalization and the discovery and mobilization of hidden energies and talents. Even in radical change, however, the actor utilizes at least some of his or her previous career competencies, for example, the self-confidence or maturity gained from previous experience. Jack found his new career through family networks, focused it through his background awareness of his ethnic identity, and added new dimensions by adapting emergent leadership skills which he had gained supervising unskilled laborers. He also rediscovered his own ambitious edge, the part of him that could not remain just a welder. He became a health aide who is not content to remain a health aide. Jack's continuing restlessness is typical of the energy of the boundaryless career.

Radical shifts may be driven by agency or communion. In agency-driven shifts the career actor seeks to enact greater control over his or her environment. Communion-focused moves, including the permanent or temporary moves of career women into maternity and child-care situations, may involve the recognition that the over-zealous pursuit of a work-based career can lead to imbalance. Jack's impatient rejection of his welding background was driven by agency, but in his developing relationships with clients and his own ethnic background he gained a new sense of communion.

Agency-driven and Communion-focused Career Shifts

Agency-driven

Dan had a successful early career as a manager in a retail chain. By the age of 25 he had a relatively senior position. But he disliked corporate life and had a strong desire to go into business for himself. He looked at the retail industry where his expertise was based, but decided the profitability would not be high enough. Instead, with two partners he set up the financial services business which provided the locus for the following 20 years of his career.

James was the manager of a recreation facility. He had been in the recreation industry for 15 years. Quite suddenly, he decided to walk away from it. He was interested in ceramic tiles, and persuaded a company selling ceramic tiles to take him on as a salesman. It was the beginning of a new career in the tiling industry.

Communion-focused

Honor, a trained and experienced nurse, trained as a teacher because she thought primary teaching work would give her hours and holidays suited to her role as a mother. But she found teaching stressful and quit her first teaching job after a few months. By then she was living with her second husband, a farmer, and working part-time on the farm. She bought into the farm, and now is a farmer, doing relief milking, farm administration, and research and development related to the dairying industry.

Isabel (introduced earlier in this chapter) has had a 15-year career in scientific research but came to feel that she was just "plodding along." Recently she took maternity leave to have her second child. A class on career paths caused her to look at herself anew. She plans to start work in a play center as an experiment in expressing her communion side at work. But "I'm sticking with the indecision and not rushing things."

Agency-driven and communion-focused

Nita rejected her parents' advice to continue her education, and drifted into temporary work – restaurant, cleaning, and factory jobs. She also had three children. Eventually, repelled by the nature of her working life, she went to university, worked her way through a degree while continuing to care for her family, earned a teaching certificate, and is now a high school teacher. Her approach to her work is informed by a deep commitment to children and to her own ethnic community.

Enterprise in Surprising Places

Much career enactment involves individual enterprise as people engage with and attempt to influence the world on their own terms. Career actors may be energetic at any age or stage of their careers. They may go through our phases of fresh energy, informed direction, and seasoned engagement in a single job, or in a series of jobs in a company or occupation, before casting off their earlier identity and pouring energy into a fresh start.

As a closing case of "Fresh Energy" – one involving many of the concepts in this chapter, including learning through travel, a self-designed apprenticeship, partner influence, and enterprise stemming from a second job – consider the case of Vera.

Nuts About Fresh Energy

Vera had a mobile childhood, with much overseas travel with her agricultural scientist father. Eventually she trained as a nurse, then married a doctor, who also travelled substantially. She had four children and brought them up. During this time her work was mainly casual, such as Red Cross teaching and teaching occupational safety. Eventually she returned to the workforce with spells in general and geriatric nursing. She and her husband bought land and a house in the country. But Vera was fired from her job in a local boarding school for "wanting to get soap in their toilets and brown bread in their diets . . . overstepping my mark."

It was a career crossroads. Vera was trying, with an associate, to develop a business in therapy workshops. She had also started growing, packaging and selling macadamia nuts when "my mum gave me two, and said, 'this is the future'." One day, in a therapy workshop, Vera's associate "indicated it was my turn and I was thinking of damn (macadamia) labels." She decided to give a full commitment to the nut business. Since then the business has grown substantially. She has 400 trees herself. Through some work at an agricultural show she found that there were many other growers in the area. They all had problems of processing and distribution, so she set up a processing unit. She employs a part-time builder to prototype equipment in her "nut-house" factory, and, more recently, a "business coach" – "because I didn't know how to run a business properly." She is getting more and more involved in added-value processing such as chocolating, and niche marketing such as corporate gifts. Her networking in the local area is extensive. At 56, Vera looks forward with hope and energy to substantial business development – good relationships with growers, secure markets, quality packaging, exports to Europe. She loves what she does. Her biggest fear: "I might die before I finish it."

While any attribution of the causes of Vera's continuous learning and energy must be speculative, we can see in her story a number of the mechanisms we have noted. She herself mentions a love of gardening and land learned from her father. In her childhood and early adulthood she seems to have been constantly "getting away," albeit at the request of others. She moved around to some extent in her work as a nurse, but it seems that her career took second place to her husband's and was focused around notions of community service rather than personal advancement or fulfillment.

But in recent years Vera has experienced a career transition of stunning magnitude. Her great oak has grown, almost literally, from a tiny acorn. She has known her own "moments of truth" when the nature of her career destiny dramatically emerged. The business has realized hidden reserves of enterprise, acumen, and joy in living. While others in their fifties are beginning to close down their careers (see Chapter 6), Vera is serving her own self-designed apprenticeship, conversing with her self-chosen mentors, developing new contacts, and facilitating the emergence not just of her own business but of a new network of interdependent ventures. She has moved from the prescribed, trained roles of nursing to her new, less constrained, role of business woman, creating opportunities for growers and employees. Her career is a prime example of enactment.

Energy Across Boundaries

In this chapter we have tried to show how boundary-crossing both demonstrates the energy of the boundary-crosser, and produces its own new productive energy through the effects of situation novelty and individual curiosity and adaptation. This applies to boundary-crossing of all types: from school to work and back; between jobs, employers, locations, industries, occupations. It is change, or the promise of change to come, that energizes career actors.

We have also begun to demonstrate how career energy begins to find direction, to move from patterns based on sensation-seeking or experimentation, to focus on better defined career objectives. Whether at the level of the project, the job, or the entire career, the novel becomes familiar, and the actor's exploration results in a sense of shape or direction. The self-designed apprenticeship lacks the bureaucratic structure of a formal apprenticeship, but increasingly the apprentice's integration of concepts and understanding of job or market define the curriculum. Career actors learn their jobs, settle into corporate or business niches, take on responsibilities for new family members and possessions, and see possible tracks to the future. The attention of career actors moves from exploring to advancing.[10] The career behavior which they enact becomes increasingly purposeful. It is to this purposefulness, this newly informed direction in which careers move, that we turn in Chapter 5.

Notes

1. Super, D.E. *The Psychology of Careers*. New York: Harper & Row, 1957; Super, D.E. A life-span, life-space approach to career development. In

D. Brown and L. Brooks (eds.) *Career Choice and Development*. San Francisco: Jossey-Bass, 1990; Super, D.E. Towards a comprehensive theory of career development. In D.H. Montross and C.J. Shinkman (eds.) *Career Development: Theory and Practice*. Springfield, IL: Charles C. Thomas, 1992, 35–64.

2. Arthur, M.B. and Kram, K.E. Reciprocity at work: the separate, yet inseparable possibilities for individual and organizational development. In M.B. Arthur, D.T. Hall, and B.S. Lawrence (eds.) *Handbook of Career Theory*. Cambridge: Cambridge University Press, 1989, pp. 292–312.

3. Super, 1992, op cit. (1), p. 42.

4. Levinson, D.J., Darrow, C.N., Klein, E.B., Levinson, M.H. and McKee, B. *The Seasons Of A Man's Life*. New York: Knopf, 1978.

5. Super, 1990, op. cit. (1).

6. Boyatzis, R.E. and Kolb, D.A. Performance, learning, and development as modes of growth and adaptation throughout our lives and careers. In M.A. Peiperl, M.B. Arthur, R. Goffee and T. Morris (eds) *Career Frontiers: New Conceptions of Working Life*. Oxford: Oxford University Press, in press.

7. Marshall, J. Living lives of change: examining the facts of women's career stories. In Peiperl et al., op. cit. (6).

8. Inkson, K., Arthur, M.B., Pringle, J.K. and Barry, S. Overseas experience versus expatriate assignment: contrasting models of human resource development. *Journal of World Business*, 1997, 4: 151–68.

9. Bardwick, J. The seasons of a woman's life. In D. McGuigan (ed.), *Women's Lives: New Theory, Research, and Policy*. Ann Arbor, Michigan: University of Michigan Center for the Continuing Education of Women, 1980, pp. 35–55.

10. Arthur and Kram op. cit. (2).

5   Informed Direction: Pursuing Career Pathways

Moving a Career

Helen trained as a nurse in her native South Africa, completing diplomas in General Nursing and Midwifery. She worked initially in hospital nursing, but soon developed an interest in occupational health and worked as an occupational health nurse for a group of five companies for several years. Then she had two children close together, during which time she had a part-time nursing job for doctors in general practice. She then took a night duty position three nights a week at a private clinic near her home. The hours suited her family commitments because "when I wasn't there my husband was there." She enjoyed working with the people in the busy medical and surgical ward, and learned as quickly as she could. Within two weeks she had supervisory responsibility for other workers. She felt good that her expertise was respected.

However, as her children grew, she did not need to continue on night duty and decided it would be a good opportunity to get back into occupational health. She took a job as a nurse in a brand new clinic in a textile factory. She had to set it up, put in procedures and processes, and train people in first aid. The workers were mainly women who were in very stressful situations. Helen found herself dealing with domestic conflict and welfare problems in a counseling situation. Although her hours were only 7.30 am to 1 p.m. it felt like full-time work. After four years she began to look for a new job.

She heard by word of mouth that a company in the automotive industry, close to her home, was looking for a new half-time nurse. She got the job. It was a great contrast to her previous job. It was a very male environment, a structured company with clear operating systems. Her boss, an engineer, was very interested in health and safety and supported her. For the first time she had a computer on her desk with relevant software in it. With the support of her company she also completed, part-time, a university diploma in occupational health.

However, Helen and her husband were feeling increasingly pressured by the violence and stress of their country. They were concerned about the possible future impact on their children, and decided to emigrate. Soon after their arrival in their new country a local employer advertised for an occupational nurse. Helen applied and, probably because of her extensive qualifications and experience, got the job from a field of 100 applicants. Initially she worked 7 a.m. to 1 p.m., but later she was asked to add three afternoon sessions at another factory in the group.

Helen sees her future mainly in terms of consolidating and extending her work with her present company. Emigrating was traumatic and she doesn't want more upheaval. Ideally, she would like not to be tied to one clinic, but instead have more of a coordinating role. She has moved a long way from her first hands-on clinical job and reflects "I have learned more in the last ten years than in my entire life."

Helen's career was focused by a general nursing qualification which she completed at its outset, and by the occupational health specialism which she took up at an early stage. If Helen experimented, she did so within the conventional parameters which her family setting and her occupational roles afforded. In her job transitions Helen has been purposeful. With each change of job she has gathered new skills, academic and industry knowledge, familiarity with new client groups, connections, and credibility. In some jobs she utilized special features of the environment to further leverage her position. As she looks back on her early career and thinks about the future, there is an almost relentless logic about her progress. Helen's is a tidy, clearly directed career.

Helen is 45. According to age/career stage theory she is at the end of the "establishment" stage of her career. If the emphasis in early career is on exploration and experiment, the emphasis in the middle career years is on finding a suitable career track or niche, and working hard at becoming "established" in it, and earning external recognition. The dominant individual need is advancement.[1]

The focus for advancement may be a particular occupation or technical skill (as in Helen's case up to now) or it may be based on an employing company (as it may be in Helen's case in the future). The old models of occupational and corporate careers come into play as individuals "seek out opportunities to become successful on the organization's – and therefore their own – behalf,"[2] in "periods of consolidation and perhaps advancement."[3] From the early thirties to the early forties, according to Levinson, men experience a distinctive period, of "becoming one's own man" during which they settle down and become a senior member of the world, including the world of work.[4] Women do not follow the same process in such a linear fashion: issues of biology, family, and multiple roles intrude, and career success as conventionally judged is less appealing.

Some women defer having children in order to compete in their careers on male terms. Other women return later in life, perhaps between ages 40 and 50, to resume full-time work, become more independent, and pursue their careers with greater vigor.[5] Helen appears to have followed this pattern. In her enactment of her career, her most important motivating force has been her concern for her family. Her career has been interrupted and has contained periods of part-time employment while she has given priority to her family. To accommodate family needs she has alternated between orthodox nursing and occupational health positions. For the sake of her family she emigrated, thereby risking a fracture of her career.

In the end, because of the thoroughness of her career preparation, she "landed on her feet," and maintained career momentum and direction. Her progress now depends on the market for her professional knowledge, her current expertise, the managerial skills which are increasingly part of her role, and the decreasing demands of her family life. Partly through choice and partly through the demands of her work, she has moved from concerns of communion, in family and hospital, to those of agency in a busy industrial company. She observes that "to be a nurse you have to have a caring attitude, but a lot of that changes when you come into the business world – you have to be more assertive." Helen has created, so far, an advancing career around the clear central theme of occupational health. In recent years she has steadily built expertise and confidence.

We call this intermediate phase, and the types of career behavior associated with it, "informed direction." Again, as recent revisions to career theory suggest, we are more interested in a particular form of behavior than in a particular career stage. Boyatzis and Kolb refer to a "performance mode" through which people may be expected to recycle, involving "preoccupation with success and . . . mastery of a job or arena of their life." The mode represents "an attempt to establish self-validation; proving yourself worthy." We found informed direction at all ages and all stages of people's careers. However, we will examine it mainly by reference to those in their middle years – mid thirties to early fifties – in whom it was most commonly represented in our sample.

As a career, job, or project unfolds, career actors tend to develop clearer direction. They begin to see ways in which broad life objectives and aspirations can be achieved. They form "couple" relationships and acquire family responsibilities which provide new opportunities for, or constraints on, career options. They make specialist choices and thereby enact the consequences of specialization into their careers. To provide control and direction in their career behavior they consciously or unconsciously rely on their past experiences, their networks, and their present situations and feelings. The data that inform their direction come not only from their paid work role but also from their wider social roles as family members, partners, parents, volunteers, members of ethnic or class groups, and positions as privileged or underprivileged members of society.

Quick Start, Enduring Legacy

The pressure to find informed direction starts early. People beginning their careers in their teens or early twenties have to make important career choices, about what kind of work to specialize in or what kind of higher education to pursue. But they have little experience to inform their judgments. They may be handicapped rather than helped by the predispositions and prejudices of parents and other advisors. The world may seem too busy and important a place to allow them the luxury of an experimental period. The pressure is often on to choose a "vocation," implicitly for life.

Right First Time

Glenda's best school subject was science, but she wanted to work with people. Her mother had a friend who was an optometrist, and Glenda considered optometry as a career choice. "It was dealing with people, it was new technology . . ., a career you could take up and do normal hours without having to do shift work, week-ends, not on call . . . a profession that not many did." Glenda enrolled for a four-year degree course. She did well academically, won prizes, and had a sponsored trip overseas. In her final year at the university she secured a one-year appointment in the local public hospital. At the end of the year she was able to move directly to a job with a local dispensing optician. She has been there over a year and is happy. "I am able to use the whole spectrum of optometry. Working in a company like that is what I planned." At 25, Glenda is settled in her professional career. "Once I decided that optometry was my chosen career, that was it. I've never regretted it and I've enjoyed it." She is married and eventually she may take a few years off work for family reasons. After that, "self-employment [as an optometrist] is an idea, the flexible hours appeal, the remuneration opportunities and the chance to be my own boss."

Glenda's entry to her career and her early progress represent a model of the way many believe career choice should work. In her early career, Glenda has practiced agency. She has pursued the mastery implied by professional qualifications and status. She chose carefully, matching her occupation to her own strengths, interests, and lifestyle preferences. She listened to advice from others. She worked hard at university and afterwards to develop her skills and strengthen her reputation. She has already established a clear professional identity. She has a good sense of what she wants. She plans realistically for the future.

Although Glenda is married, her choices are as yet relatively unaffected by family responsibilities. As long as she and her husband can pursue their professional directions in good jobs in the city in which they live, work-career decisions can be based on work-career issues. But as Glenda herself realizes, that situation is unlikely to be permanent. Families change things. Informed direction must take account of the career actor's wider social roles and obligations.

Teaming Up and Trying Out

Most career actors are married or in live-in relationships by the age of 30. Often, their partners are also pursuing full-time careers. The mobility of the career actor becomes tied to the mobility of the partner.

The intertwining of relationships with career direction and progress was evident in a number of cases. Participants travelled overseas with partners or met them there. Career decisions are influenced by the compatibility of options with partners' careers. The communion of a good personal relationship may mitigate the agency of work and career behavior in competitive employment settings. Some career actors talked about the value of a supportive partner in assisting their careers, guiding their decision-making, or giving them confidence to accept new challenges. In other cases, partners' careers were seen to have some influence over career decisions.

Partners' Influence on Early Careers

Barbara, a physical therapist, met and married her husband in Canada while travelling overseas. He moved to a job in Britain, and she searched the city he was located in until she found a suitable job.

Jeff's low-paid self-designed apprenticeship as a landscaper was made possible by his wife's sympathy with his situation and her willingness to be the primary wage-earner (as a teacher) until he became established.

Catherine (Chapter 2) was working for a large telecommunications company when her husband got a promotion to a new location. She campaigned against an unsympathetic boss for a transfer and was eventually offered a suitable job.

Damien (Chapter 3), the chef, had a period of excessive hours and self-induced stress. His wife suggested he take a stress management course, and he found it changed his life. When he went overseas with his wife, they worked in tandem managing the kitchen of an English pub.

Family First

The establishment of the Industrial State created a division between the private and public spheres. The resultant interplay between home and paid work responsibilities has been an issue ever since. The conflicts around managing the home–work intersection, and particularly the family, have been exacerbated with the awakening and the questioning of social roles which grew out of the women's movement of the 1970s. Fletcher and Bailyn[6] refer to the home–work divide as the "last boundary" in a world of boundaryless work.

Many women have a clear sense of direction which comes with a traditional female role and a personal desire to place their family in a central position in their lives. Several years ago, it was suggested that any career theory for women should include consideration of career preparation, the influence of marriage and children, the age of women, and differential opportunities for women and men in the workplace and wider society.[7] These factors still resonate.

Traditional career theory is biased towards men's experiences. By treating the careers of middle-class men as normative, it has distorted our understanding of women and their lives.[8] At the same time it has presented a narrow and limited view of men's lives: that men tend to pursue conventional career advancement from an early age. For women, a more likely pattern is a push to committed relationships and decisions about children in the early adult years, followed by increased assertiveness and work accomplishment nearer to middle adulthood.[9] In contrast, middle adulthood is a time which is likely to be a period of major reassessment of men's life goals (the well-known "mid-life crisis") illustrated in our sample by Dan's dramatic shift from agency to communion (Chapter 3).

However, the orderliness predicted by stage theorists for women's and men's lives is increasingly problematic because of the fragmentation of linear careers in the emerging boundaryless work environment. It is possible that, in the world of discontinuous systems of work, the interruptions and improvisations which have always been characteristic of women's careers will become more common in all careers. In addition, many women are becoming more assertive in seeking to pursue careers in a similar manner to men, with a minimum of interruption by child-care considerations and a more equal sharing of responsibilities with their male partners.

It may be advantageous to some career actors (principally men) and some companies to maintain the boundary, and as far as possible to create a mode of thought and action, where work and career decisions are made without reference to family considerations. However, it was clear that the careers of the majority of our career actors had been affected in their direction and their momentum by family considerations. This was particularly true of women's careers, and of phases of career where there were young children living at home. As women described their careers, talk of children was woven seamlessly into their narrative as they described the job terminations, part-time hours, relocations of workplace, child-care arrangements, complementarity with their husbands' shifts, and arrangements when children were ill.

A striking feature was the cohort effect on the timing of children in the lives of these women. Women over 40 and those of non-Caucasian ethnicity tended to have given priority to their home life, and had fitted paid work around maternity, child-rearing, and other domestic responsibilities. This is epitomized by Nita, who has three children, and for whom parenting "is still the important influencing factor up until today." Women in their late twenties and early thirties deliberately planned when they would have a baby (often to the month) and how it would fit in with work and other goals. Also striking was the low proportion of younger women in the sample who had children. This reflects a trend in many developed countries.

These family accommodations were a central part of women's careers. In some cases, even where the woman had worked full-time for several years, the career was relatively unimportant: it was no more than a backdrop or a prop to the primary, family-centered, continuation of their lives. However, such a mode needs to be thought of not as an interruption to career, but as a special kind of career experience. In such cases it is family life rather than work that provides the career, the accumulation of learning, the reciprocities between individual and social institution, and the spirals of personal development.

Family First

Elsie is an office administrator who has drawn boundaries around work from which she tries to protect her home life. Early in her work life she moved companies to follow opportunities. After she married and had

children, family matters were always the primary criterion for career decisions. When her job moved to a location less convenient to her home and
the hours extended to interfere with her family life, she resigned, remaining
unemployed for several months as she sought local part-time work in a
recession. She finally obtained her present job seven minutes drive from
her home, "a very big plus." Her children have now grown up and left
home, but her career orientation has not changed. Her primary objective is
quality of life with her husband. The key recurring themes in her career
experience are location and hours of work. Her work career is bounded
by, and subservient to, her home life.

Annette recognizes that she is fortunate not to have to work full time
and, since early training and practice as a primary school teacher, has
had little engagement with the world of paid work. "He didn't want me
to work full-time . . . nor did I really." Annette is the only woman in the
sample who fulfils the traditional homemaker role through choice.

However, another common pattern for women[10] is that their preoccupation with committed relationships and decisions about children in the early adult years is followed nearer middle adulthood by
increased assertiveness and work accomplishment. Vera, the macadamia nut grower (Chapter 4), is an example. Helen the occupational
health nurse is another. In our sample, schoolteacher Nita and school
counsellor Janice, had also accelerated their careers after child-rearing
in ways that were informed and energized by the child-rearing/
home-making experience.

The Family Man

Concern about the balance between home and family is overwhelm-
ingly a women's issue, because both men and women tend to hold
the expectation that women are primarily responsible for the well-
being of the home and family. This responsibility becomes sharpened
when children arrive and in our sample, with the exception of one
man, it was the women's careers that had been changed to accommodate the children.

In contrast to women's characteristic family-centered career talk,
many men in the sample did not mention their spouses or family
except in response to the direct demographic questions. It is difficult
to judge from their responses whether their families had a major role
in their choices around work. It appeared that the family acted as a
backdrop, a presence in the background of their work activity.
Perhaps family and career were viewed as important, but essentially

separate, activities. In general, younger men and those of non-Caucasian ethnicity spoke more of their partners and children. In only a few cases was there evidence of clear career adjustments being made to accommodate family needs.

More Family, Less Work

Oliver's career took him abroad for much of the time. The separation from his family became "untenable," so he quit a successful career track, and moved into lower-level work, where he was able to capitalize on some of his technical knowledge. Essentially he began a second career for the sake of his family relationships.

Henry is from an ethnic minority which attributes great importance to the extended family. Because of the way he was brought up, he keenly feels a responsibility to his family. Separated from his immediate family by overseas work, he realized how much they really meant to him, "like a can of Coke on a hot day." He came home to his family and a period of unemployment.

Darren has continued the family line of truck driving for years and although only 26 is settling down. He realized that although his elder daughter was five years old he only saw her half the time. He does not want his children to become truck drivers but to do "something more meaningful [where] you can have a more suitable home life."

Sharing the Business of Living

A common way of resolving home–work conflict is through complementarity, rather than a sharing of the roles in a domestic partnership. One way of resolving the tension that is created for a relationship by child-care demands and the wish of the partners to spend time together is for the partners to combine their energies and talents in a "family business." If the venture is home-based, child-care problems can be addressed; even if it is not, partners can take work home or alternate their hours to provide child-care. Farming provides one example where, traditionally, men and women contribute complementary interests and skills. In other cases, women may be expected to provide secretarial or clerical assistance to ventures based on the man's technical expertise or enterprise. Joint ownership of a small shop or café is another common model. But these models may share a rather limited view of women's abilities and aspirations as contributors to the venture. Women are becoming increasingly assertive in pursuing their careers as expressions of personal fulfillment rather than as practical support to a partner.[11]

The following examples indicate both problems and effective accommodations when partners try to share their careers around their own ventures.

Working and Living Together

Honor initially became qualified as a nurse, but later trained as a teacher because she thought the hours of work in teaching would make it easier to find time for her family's needs. But she found teaching unexpectedly stressful. By this time she was living with her second husband, a farmer, on his farm. She quit teaching and started working part-time on the farm. Now she has become a financial partner, and does relief milking, calving, administration, and research and development. She works cooperatively with her husband to develop the farm and takes part in professional farming activities. She also works one day a week as a clinic nurse. Through her relationship with her husband, Honor has successfully integrated her work life and family life, and has also established a new career.

Vandanna is in partnership with her husband and they run the business from home. She is telephone receptionist, does the typing, and some selling. In the quieter moments "I spend time with my little one [15 months] and catch up with the housework. . . . So I am looking after the business and the family."

Jean followed her husband as he relocated with his air force career. On his discharge they acquired the first of a series of small businesses - dairies and lunch bars. After investing much time, energy, and considerable capital into the business, it was caught in a recession, and they eventually sold it at a loss. Jean won't go back into self-employment because her husband doesn't want to, "and we do everything together."

Paula had developed her business career and held an executive position. However, her husband persuaded her to leave it to come and provide administrative support to the family business, thus "keeping it in the family" rather than recruiting an outsider. Paula found the environment of the family business unpleasant and dirty, and her work unstimulating. Eventually she talked her husband into selling the business, and has now resumed her career with another company.

The "True Vocationalist"

Family and home typically set parameters for the direction a career actor will pursue. Specific direction comes more frequently from occupation. Glenda's decision, while still a teenager, to train as an optometrist, is a case in point. In so doing, she made a huge investment of her time, her energy, and herself in a specific form of career identity. Similarly, Helen's choice of nursing, and subsequently occupational health nursing, provided absolute clarity of career identity. In Helen's case, the investment appears to be paying off.

Occupational choice represents a popular model for understanding careers. As children we are not asked, "Who are you going to work for when you leave school?" or "What do you hope to learn after you leave school?", but "What are you going to be (or do) when you leave school?" Often, the unspoken assumption appears to be, "for the rest of your life." This is where occupation becomes vocation.

Being Called

Nigel, following experience as a primary teacher, went to theological college, graduated in his late twenties, and became a minister of religion. He has been minister of his present parish for eight years. He talks about his "vocation." He feels multiple, sometimes conflicting, obligations, to the Church, to its hierarchy, to his parishioners, and to his family. He sees very clearly the contradictions of his position: "On the one hand the assumption is that you will keep the numbers up . . . on the other hand any faithfulness to the record of the Christian Church will in fact deter people." He worries that "the structure of society is eroding." He has "cycles of doubt, cycles of evaluation" and has applied for non-pastoral jobs in the church. But he has support networks of other clergy with whom he has worked.

Nigel does not like the word "career." It "implies a career structure and in my perception that is not important for clergy. . . . I believe we are called to fulfil a vocation, not to climb a career tree." His job is "to be faithful." "I have signed my life away in faithfulness . . . to the church." Nigel sees no upward or onward trajectory for the future. Nigel's advice to young people is to "facilitate your self-discovery rather than shaping your life."

Nigel's career is ongoing communion; agency is left largely to God. The word "vocation" which Nigel uses is from the Latin *vocare*, "to call." God calls his individual servants to a place in the world where they play their part, serving him and his people. In colloquial speech, "vocation" means an occupation towards which the individual is drawn, implicitly for a lifetime. "Vocation" tends to refer to professional occupations in which one must make substantial investments to join, in the expectation of a long-term commitment, and, as in the ministry, serving people: for example, medicine, nursing, teaching, and law.

The concept "vocation" is also a strong element in our historic Industrial State culture of stability. Vocation provides a means to stabilize and specialize human expertise. It encourages individuals to conceive of their identity in single-occupation terms – "I'm a carpenter," "I'm a nurse" – and to utilize their qualifications and experience efficiently within the spheres for which they were intended. The career may be linear – the person simply acquires greater expertise in the same specialization. But it may also be circular or spiral, as the core qualification or expertise becomes a reference point around which the career actor moves to acquire a wider range of knowledge. Occupational careers encourage career actors to observe occupational norms and professional standards. Terms such as "vocational choice," and "vocational counselling," focused on young people as they make early career decisions, imply once-and-for-all investment in a single occupation.

Nigel's story is truly vocational, and it is supported by a vocational script provided by the Church. He has invested much of his being in his occupation. While learning is acknowledged, the idea of ongoing communion through service and faith overwhelms any sense of progress in the conventional sense: Nigel is contemptuous of the idea. The sense of identity that comes from his communion with God and his ministerial role is so strong that neither the hierarchical organizational career nor the lateral boundaryless career are possibilities. Significantly, Nigel makes good use of his occupational community of other clergy to help him to maintain his morale in the midst of the difficult contradictions of his role.

As organizational boundaries dissolve, and as careers increasingly move between organizations, one consequence that has been forecast is "the increased centrality of occupations as the primary loci of individual careers."[12] The occupation has always held an important place as a source of personal identity and self-esteem, and as an organizing principle around which to construct careers. This is borne out by the results we reported in Chapter 2, showing that 41 percent of our sample had been in the same occupation for the ten years on which we focused, and a further 15 percent for at least five years.

Long-term occupations remain important stabilizing institutions. Most "vocational" career actors had made substantial investments in vocational education and training. Their formal qualifications and accumulated experience provided them with competence and value in the labor market. In addition, many participants clearly enjoyed their occupations and their mastery of their own specialist spheres.

Nevertheless, occupations are continuously redefined. Qualification arrangements are liberalized, opening reserved occupations to outsiders. Standards of practice are changed, and practitioners are required to satisfy new criteria. The market or the clientele of the occupation may change over time. In the recent convergence of banking, insurance, real estate financing, and other financial services, vocationalists such as bankers, insurance salespeople, and realtors may have to operate in an alien environment, in which their training may seem at best limited and at worst irrelevant. Members must constantly update their skills in order to retain membership of the occupational group and relevant competence in a changing world. Pitfalls as well as principles for making one's investment in an occupation pay off are considered in Chapter 6.

Growing with the Company

An alternative – and sometimes an addition – to investing in an occupation, is investing in a company or other employing institution. Many career actors use an occupational qualification or experience in order to obtain work in a company, and then advance their careers by continuing to develop a "mutual loyalty" contract with their employer. Through the reciprocities described in Chapter 1, career actors and employers engage in a dynamic, developing exchange. From a careers perspective we can track the reciprocal relationships unfolding continuously over time. As the company builds its human capital and thereby its knowledge base, the career actor simultaneously accumulates learning valuable to both company and career. But the arrangement may be a lop-sided one. For example, an individual may pour energy into developing a technology that has a limited life-span and is specific to one company. Or a company may provide leading-edge expertise or valuable client information to an employee who plans to join a competitor or start her or his own business.

It is open to each party, at any time, to withdraw its investment in the other. Rational calculation can provide a basis for continuation of, change to, or termination of, the relationship. In practice, sentiment about past exchanges – for example, company gratitude to a long-service employee, or employee love for the technical intricacies of the job – may moderate rational decision-making. Under these circumstances, reciprocal benefit can be replaced by possibly unintentional exploitation.

Investing in a company is probably riskier than investing in an occupation. One of the largest corporations in the world, IBM, was synonymous with lifetime employment before "shocking" its employees and the world with massive workforce reductions in the late 1980s and early 1990s.[13] In recent years downsizing and restructuring have caused many staff to lose their jobs despite all their expectations of career security. Yet, for many, finding and retaining a long-term niche within a benevolent company remains a powerful goal. And some companies still try to look after staff in the expected manner.

Confident in the Company

Lily is a member of an ethnic minority whose family has always been involved in factory work. Her first work experience after leaving school was to follow her aunt into a job at a local factory, mainly lifting and carrying. She was shy and lacked confidence, which caused her to fear change and to doubt if she could ever do better. But during a break from work looking after her small children she took a three-month subsidized course in clerical work. Her job counsellor encouraged her to apply for a job as an accounts clerk in a local supermarket chain.

Now aged 32, Lily has been with the supermarket company eight years. She now does an expanded job, and has learned computer skills. She enjoys her work, particularly her relationship with supportive colleagues, "a great bunch of people." She reports having more confidence, and even speaking up at meetings. But she has no plans to change from her present position or company, and offers that "I can never see myself moving on."

In the type of niche which Lily found, the work environment is congenial, new learning is possible, and the developing reciprocity with the employer is functional. Nevertheless, a key issue for career actors is the nature of their investment. Cultivating a "mutual loyalty" contract with an employer is attractive, for it provides apparent security and the comfort of the familiar. But career actors need to be aware that in the end their contract is not with the "great bunch of people" they work with, or their immediate supervisors, but with a formally constituted legal entity – the employer. Forces beyond a company's control may force restructuring involving abrupt termination of a mutually beneficial career accommodation. Peter (Chapter 1) and Gus (Chapter 3) were able to bring enough learning out of the relationship to turn such situations to their advantage. As we shall see in Chapter 6, not all career actors are so fortunate.

Direction Through Idealism

A more basic source of career direction is personal values. Personal values are often reflected, of course, in the relationship of work career to family concerns, or in the occupation or company in which actors choose to make their career investments. But values may have an even more direct expression in career behavior.

A number of the people in the sample had a growing awareness of ethnic or class injustices which had provided direction to their careers. Their own diverse experiences were a strong impetus for action, on behalf of others as well as themselves. Most of these were women.

Fighting Against Injustice

Julie worked in a fast-food chain and got involved in the unions there "because we were the hardest hit" namely the young, part-time, marginalized workforce. Julie's mother, who had been involved in the union while she had worked as a cleaner, was a powerful role model. Julie has been influenced by her observation of poor work conditions in booming businesses, and by the fear of unemployment which has affected many of her friends. Julie performed her role as occasional union representative at her workplace to such effect that the union offered her a full-time job as an organizer. She has now been doing the job for two years.

Nita initially rejected her middle-class parents' advice to seek formal qualifications, so she left school and became a waitress. She had three children, while scratching together a living by doing cleaning and factory work. Ten years into her work career, she decided to study, went to university and trained as a teacher. Her first teaching job was in a "very white, upper-middle-class school." Her visible presence as a member of an ethnic minority "forced the staff to see a different point of view" and she became aware of herself being perceived as a token for her ethnic group. Nita then moved to a school in a poorer part of the city and understood that having enough to eat affects the children's ability to learn. Through her teaching she began to see that the education system had failed working-class children of her own ethnicity. It was a real lesson, "Now, I am much more willing, if it doesn't work, get something else and try it." She is openly contemptuous of patronizing European teachers, and of token minority participation. She believes career progress is reserved for those who "nod their heads up and down." Although she hopes that her career progression will eventually enable her "to study, research and travel," her career behavior is vitally informed by her personal mission to improve the education of her people. She feels a major conflict in supporting and working in a system she does not respect.

Julie's story is affected by her trade union family background and her early work experiences in an industry largely staffed by unskilled temporary workers. Nita's has been vitally influenced by her role as a single parent and as a member of her ethnic community. Her cultural and political awareness informs her direction, and while she takes pride in having obtained qualifications and having a secure job, there are major conflicts for her in supporting and working in a system that she does not respect, and between her work and non-work roles.

The stories of Julie and Nita demonstrate a developing sense of direction in their life courses which was sparked by a sharpening awareness of their gender and their class or ethnic identity. The chosen direction is not solely for individual ambition or personal gain but has become intertwined with a sense of social responsibility. They demonstrate agency linked with communion. Their strong agentic action is focused on helping the collective groups of which they are members. In their careers we see strong, purposeful direction with important interplays between agency and communion, as well as individual and collective action.

Purpose Through Volunteering

Another source of career direction – or often, redirection – is what we might call the "second strings" of people's bows: activities which start quietly, in the spare corners of their lives – in their volunteer service activities, hobbies, and their part-time second jobs. Such activities may start as tiny fragments, counterpoints to the "serious work" of the main job or career. They may then prove so enlivening to the individual that they become options for major career development.

Volunteering provides an outlet for personal values which may not be fully satisfied in the family setting or in a paid job. It also provides a vehicle for balancing agency and communion. For a few of our participants involvement in the voluntary sector was a key for them to find direction in their careers.

Volunteering for Good

Jennie was a full-time homemaker for twenty years, during which time she had extensive volunteer experience in nursery school, school committees, the Red Cross, and other institutions. She volunteered to work with a disability service, engaged in some relief teaching, job-shared with her daughter, and then moved from volunteer worker to paid manager of a facility, to self-employed provider of disability services.

Christine volunteered to work with the disabled at school and later volunteered to work with the blind. She pursued a clerical career but became more and more interested in helping the disabled. Eventually she left her job, and is currently a student in a two-year course which will enable her teach people with disabilities. She realizes that once she graduates and gets a full-time job in her chosen career she will be worse off financially, but she hopes to "benefit the people I will be working with."

Evelyn's commitment to volunteer work far outweighs her commitment to paid work. She has had a 22-year career in volunteer work, and "can't see myself stopping." She recently acquired a full-time paid position in an import business, but only took it to help out a friend, and still spends 15 hours per week in Scouting and in a child welfare agency. She is a district representative and has won numerous merit and achievement awards for her service, time and positions of responsibility. In spite of her recently acquired paid work, she identified herself as a "voluntary worker" as her occupation, and it was the unpaid work she chose to discuss in her employment history interview. It is easy to imagine that if she had to choose between paid and unpaid work, it would be the paid work that would go.

Through the unpaid work of volunteering, Jennie and Christine have found paid careers. Volunteer work has been a way for them to identify interests and strengths, and to develop skills. Their careers provide elements of altruism which are clearly important to them. For Evelyn her volunteer work *is* her career. It is there and in her family that she has developed important skills and knowledge, which now, almost inadvertently, she is able utilize in the import business.

For other members of our sample, volunteer work was frequently mentioned as a means of expressing personal values, or a way of returning something to the community, or a source of balance in their lives. A few recognized clear career advantages emerging from their volunteer activities. For example, businessman Cedric had done free professional work for volunteer groups and had noticed that this work gave him "an immediate profile" in his business, where reputation by word of mouth is crucial to business development. In contrast, most of the women with children did volunteer work around their children's school activities, apparently as a matter of course. Several commented on wider career benefits such as increased self-confidence and administrative skills, but such acquisitions were apparently serendipitous rather than planned. Even from this sample it is easy to appreciate the huge contribution that women make in the volunteer sector, and the ways in which the skills developed can lead to wider career development and paid positions.

The Enterprising Second Job

Regular employment does not always provide the career opportunities people seek, and for many workers self-employment seems out of range. Restrictive employment conditions may not provide scope for people's enterprising energy. A common approach, reported by about half of our participants at some stage of their careers, is to try to do something extra in one's own time.

Leveraging Hobbies

Tony, a welder, has started a part-time business with his brother-in-law, making and selling biscuits from an ethnic recipe. Tony's share of the revenue amounts to one-third of his regular job earnings, and the business is expanding.

Elaine (Chapter 4), a court registrar, does telemarketing from home in the evenings. Her talent is such that in a few hours a week she can make more money than in her full-time job.

Catherine (Chapter 2) when a bank employee, invested one night a week in tutoring undergraduates in marketing. Subsequently she was able to use the experience to gain a full-time lecturing position in an expanding higher education program.

Cedric was a senior manager who tried to establish a business in computer consumables in his spare time. When he was laid off he capitalized on the experience, buying an established business in a related field. This now provides him with a good standard of living and a more relaxed lifestyle.

We have already covered other examples: Albert, the part-time barman whose bar work led to a possible life-changing business opportunity; Brett, the plasterer, who is also a part-time actor and musician; Jack, the health assistant, who mentioned in passing that he was trying to make additional income by trading in gold coins. Already these workers have fitted enterprise into their lives alongside regular employment. Other ideas are in participants' consciousness but not yet developed: Gail, a plateaued office employee, toys with ideas of accounting and pottery, for running a business from home. What other ideas do participants have that are so insubstantial that they do not mention them?

As careers are enacted, the dream of enterprise is a potent force for fresh energy. However, the focus on enterprise has its dark side. Self-employment can be humdrum and enslaving. As will be detailed in Chapter 6, a few members of our sample recalled periods of involvement in small personal or family businesses which brought long hours and little money. They were glad to escape.

Moving About the Chessboard

The problem with the term "direction" as a chapter heading is that it can appear to imply linearity. It might be thought that after the initial, exploratory phase, careers somehow acquire "direction" and proceed without deviation towards it. Thus, the family, occupation, or company, may be seen as guides, beacons, or even boundaries within which the career proceeds.

Indeed that was true of many of our sample. Helen the occupational nurse, Nigel the minister, and Lily the supermarket clerk were among those whose careers were set apparently on "railroad tracks" of clear direction. Such workers are heavily represented in this chapter because that is the chapter's nature. But nearly all of them – including Helen, Nigel, and Lily – had histories such that their present tracks might not have been at all predictable from an earlier inspection. And how many of the tracks apparent in our career actors today will we find, if we return in five or ten years, to have disappeared or turned through seemingly impossible angles? In the length of time a career takes, with the personal and role changes that the career actor undergoes, in the cauldron of change that is the current career environment, it is not reasonable to expect stability in direction.

Many of the stories in this chapter are of actors who have clear direction for now, but who have come from long periods of trial-and-error experimentation, ambiguous direction, and energetic movement in directions quite different from the one now being taken. Different principles of direction govern the career at different times. Consider some of the young professional people whose careers we have covered in some detail in this and earlier chapters.

Spiralling

Peter (Chapter 1) invested successively in an occupation (computer programming), overseas travel and experience, a company, a succession of broadening lateral moves within the company, and finally an entrepreneurial opportunity. No move has involved a major increase in status. Each has leveraged previous experience but also involved movement to a new type of work. Peter has "circled" his way to a position of considerable responsibility and reward.

Susan (Chapter 1) used an occupational qualification in food technology to gain employment and credibility in the food industry, then food
industry experience to move laterally into a new occupation, marketing.
Her marketing expertise freed her to move into new industries. Like Peter,
she enhanced her experience and prospects through overseas travel. She
now has a professional identity which she seeks to extend into new fields.

Catherine (Chapter 2) has for much of her career had a broad goal of
moving away from her accounting specialization into a career as a broad-
based marketing professional. She used employment in a higher education
institution to "learn the ropes," both theoretical and practical. She used her
"junior marketer" status in a telecommunications company to learn different facets of the role through a succession of engineered lateral moves.
Having reached the objective of being marketing manager for a small
company, she is now reviewing her options and planning further extension
of her learning.

Damien's career (Chapter 3) as a chef is driven by a love of his
occupation and a desire to learn the widest possible range of skills within it.
In his early years he exhibited "loyalty" to a main employer but departed
from it periodically, making lateral shifts to other restaurants from which he
believed he could learn. Characteristically for the catering industry, he has
had a highly mobile "boundaryless" career. Over time, he has started to
acquire management positions.

A suitable metaphor here is of self-moving and self-learning pieces
on a chessboard. The pieces start with limited movement available to
them, but as they move they acquire not only new positions but the
potential for a wider range of new moves. The objective of the game
is hazy rather than fixed but becomes clearer as new experiences and
knowledge are gathered. Often, as with Gus's "knight's move" when
he surprisingly acquired an enterepreneurial interest in what had
been his old mundane job, the moves are enacted opportunistically
rather than planned rationally in advance. From time to time,
direction, at least for the short-term, clarifies itself into sharp focus
before diffusing again into a swirling mist of different possibilities.
Moves on the board may be hard-headedly rational or whimsically
experimental.

As the career actors move on through the years, past experience
becomes an asset or a burden that is harder and harder to ignore. At
the different levels – project, job, career – investments accumulate,
identity crystallizes, and reciprocities shape and limit future possibilities. Wide upward spirals may flatten out into ever-decreasing
circles or dull plateaus. Liveliness gives way to familiar routines and
occupational life loses its "spice." Meantime, alternative stimulation
or stress may come from the external environment of work or the
changing social roles of the actor. Agentic career actors may yearn

for more communion in their lives. At such a point, perhaps, the key career issue becomes one of holding on, or "stewardship."[14] It is to this phase of the project, job, and career cycle that we turn in Chapter 6.

Notes

1. Arthur, M.B. and Kram, K.E. Reciprocity at work: the separate, yet inseparable possibilities for individual and organizational development. In M.B. Arthur, D.T. Hall, and B.S. Lawrence (eds.) *Handbook of Career Theory.* Cambridge: Cambridge University Press, 1989, pp. 292–312.

2. ibid., p. 295.

3. Super, D.E. Towards a comprehensive theory of career development. In D.H. Montross and C.J. Shinkman (eds.) *Career Development: Theory and Practice.* Springfield, IL: Charles C. Thomas, 1992.

4. Levinson, D.J. A conception of adult development. *American Psychologist*, 1986, 41 (1): 3–13.

5. Gallos, J.V. Exploring women's development: implications for career theory, practice, and research. In M.B. Arthur, D.T. Hall, and B.S. Lawrence (eds.) *Handbook of Career Theory.* New York: Cambridge University Press, 1989, pp. 110–32.

6. Fletcher, J.K. and Bailyn, L. Challenging the last boundary: reconnecting work and family. In M.B. Arthur and D.M. Rousseau, *The Boundaryless Career: A New Employment Principle for a New Organizational Era.* New York: Oxford University Press, 1996, 256–67.

7. Larwood, L. and Gutek, B. (eds.) *Women's Career Development.* Newbury Park, CA: Sage, 1987.

8. Gallos, J.V. Exploring women's development: implications for career theory, practice, and research. In Arthur, Hall and Lawrence, op. cit. (1).

9. Bardwick, J. The seasons of a woman's life. In D. McGuigan (ed.) *Women's Lives: New Theory, Research, and Policy.* Ann Arbor: University of Michigan Center for Continuing Education of Women, 1980, pp. 35–55.

10. Gallos, op. cit. (5).

11. Ornstein, S., and Isabella, L. Age versus stage models of career attitudes of women: a partial replication and extension. *Journal of Vocational Behavior*, 1990, (36): 1–19; Pringle, J.K. Re-thinking careers: in for life. In L. Lord, A. Kinnear, F. McKenzie and L. Pike, *International Women in Leadership Conference Proceedings.* Perth: Edith Cowan University, 1995, pp. 15–22.

12. Tolbert, P.C. Occupations, organizations, and boundaryless careers. In Arthur and Rousseau, op. cit. (6), pp. 331–49.

13. See, for example *Time*, The humbling of a computer colossus, May 20, 1991, p. 42 and Big Blue's Blues, October 12, 1992, p. 29.

14. Arthur and Kram, op. cit. (1).

6 Seasoned Engagement: Rounding Out Career Experience

Holding On in a Changing World

Oliver's career has been as a technical specialist with high qualifications in his field. He spent much of his early career travelling internationally. When his company was taken over his career prospects deteriorated and he joined a ship management company, still living in one country but working from a base in another and still doing much overseas travel.

When he was about 40 Oliver's way of life became incompatible with his family commitments. He wanted his wife and children to be settled in one place and he wanted to live with them rather than visiting them as often as he could. He thought the commercial side of his industry would be interesting. He contacted an old friend in an overseas insurance business with a local office, was offered a job (again based on his specialist qualifications and experience), and returned to his home country, dropping his salary substantially. He worked in insurance for three years, increasing his knowledge and making good industry contacts. He wanted to become a partner in the business, but did not get along well with one of the other partners.

A few years ago Oliver moved to an educational job in his home area, in a training agency associated with his industry, where he teaches the technical subjects which have provided the basis of his career. When the agency was reorganized as a higher education institution, Oliver stayed on as a lecturer. It was a bad move from a geographical point of view, requiring a long commute from the home he loved. But his strong background and good industry networks are very helpful, and there is a lot of "we" feeling in his unit. He has had various projects, the latest being the development of a new diploma program, and he looks forward to new challenges.

His department's market focus has shifted from technical and legal matters, to a more commercial emphasis, with a developing customer base among people from related industries. His institution expects the unit to be economically viable, and that is a threat. There is strong competition for educational customers. At 53, Oliver feels vulnerable. His job is increasingly concerned with marketing and administration. It takes a lot of time, and is very stressful. His wife has suggested he should leave, but there are few options: he's not sure he wants to return to insurance. The possibility of losing his job is something "I've put in a compartment and not thought about because of its difficulty." But once his current project is over he hopes to wind down, read some English and philosophy, and enjoy more recreation time.

Oliver's career demonstrates the difficulty of combining a career with family development. He is particularly skilled in adapting to an increasingly commercial ethos in an educational unit, but he is resentful that despite his efforts he is still stressed and still vulnerable. As he himself puts it: "Unemployment [has been] a major concern. My age, 53, places me in an invidious position of being unlikely to get employment again."

Oliver built a solid career base from his technical qualifications and has continued to adapt his industry knowledge and experience to meet the changing requirements of industry restructuring and his wish for a suburban family life in his home city, uncomplicated by the need for extensive travel. As he has developed his career around his technical base, he has continued to learn, and has engaged productively with each new challenge. But adaptive as Oliver has been, it is beginning to seem as though the world has changed and restructured too fast for him. His qualifications – obtained over 20 years ago – and his emergent experience seem increasingly marginalized in a specialist educational role in an institution whose market is changing. He has neither the opportunity nor the wish to return to previous types of work. His lack of versatility leaves him vulnerable. His career has become a matter of "holding on."

Age/stage theorists would recognize Oliver. Super calls middle age, from 45 to 65, the "maintenance" stage,[1] and discusses how career actors are intent on preserving the places they have made in the world. Super calls it "holding one's own."[2] A common parallel concern is captured by what Erikson calls "generativity" towards other, typically younger, members of society.[3] The broad tasks of this stage have been described as follows:

> In the mature career years, individuals are generally faced with the tasks of securing and maintaining their emergent status, experiencing continued affirmation of their work, and passing on the benefits of their learning to others . . . [S]ince there are dual components of taking care of self as well as others . . . the individual need associated with [these tasks may be labelled] *protecting*.[4]

It is evident from Oliver's case that protection may well be necessary. It is not necessarily easy to maintain one's position when flexibility and future options are declining, amid great forces of change, in technology, in competitive requirements, and in surrounding structures. Super notes the threat to mature people of "the competition of younger men and women."[5] Moreover, the great restructurings of enterprise may cause a "restructuring of aspirations,"[6] in which mature career actors "rest on their oars . . . [and] go through the routines of paperwork, but avoid learning opportunities." Others, as Super observes, "make a point of keeping up to date" or even "handle their careers as though they were still at the establishment phase, breaking new ground."[7] In other words, they cycle back to the exploring, novelty-seeking phase that we detailed in Chapter 4, which was so nicely illustrated by Vera, 56-year-old macadamia nut grower.

Boyatzis and Kolb's third mode of career adaptation (after the learning and performance modes already discussed in the preceding chapters) is what they call the "development mode." In this, people are focused on "fulfillment of their purpose, or calling, in terms of a specific agenda." The agenda may relate to a whole career, or the concluding part of a particular career cycle. In accepting the usefulness of a "stage" approach as a basis for classifying diverse career data, we must not fall into the trap of stereotyping.

The major asset of mature career actors is usually their experience. They build this over the first half of a career and seek to leverage it for their long-term protection and further development. At the same time, the changing circumstances of the economic world, people's non-work roles, their changing physical and mental capabilities, their family circumstances, and their motives, continue to provide new challenges. A key issue in this chapter is the security, for single-occupation, single-industry, and long-service company employees, of investing in institution-bound experience. What happens, in the end, to immobile people in a mobile society?

We consider here how the informed direction outlined in Chapter 5, often fuelled by the fresh energy described in Chapter 4, plays out over the long term. We term this phase "seasoned engagement." It is given its own special character by the career actor's unique accumulated experience. Although, for the moment, we apply the notion of seasoned engagement at the level of the career, the same ideas of "holding on," "experiencing affirmation," and "passing on learning to others" can apply at the level of job, or project. However, it is the mature career actors in our sample, those in their late forties and over, with whom this chapter is mainly concerned.

The Perils of Vocationalism

In Chapter 5 we described how many career actors establish direction for their lives by investing in one of two career institutions:

occupation and company. Glenda, the optometrist, is an example of those who have made primary investments in professional occupations and vocations, while Lily, the supermarket clerk, made a major investment in her company. However, Glenda and Lily were young women at a relatively early stage in their careers. As we hinted in Chapter 5, tying one's fate too securely to the fortunes of a fallible institution may be a risky strategy. The risk may become apparent, however, only in the fullness of time.

Building a strong occupational identity is a two-edged sword. On the one hand, the cultivation of valued occupational skills can be a means of high earnings, strong career growth, and protection against the decline of a specific employer. On the other hand, good occupational experience and qualifications cannot be expected to provide indefinite career security. Norman's story is a cautionary tale.

Sidelined

Norman, as a young man in the early 1960s, gained good qualifications in accountancy. He was ambitious and assumed that eventually he would occupy a senior business position. But a different pattern developed. As he moved from job to job in the financial services industry, Norman tended to find himself marginalized from real power in the companies he worked for, and would move on. His last resignation took place nearly ten years ago, shortly before a major crash in the stock market.

Suddenly, Norman found, at 46 years of age, that he was unemployed. At first he assumed this was an effect of an economy in recession. In due course the economy picked up, yet Norman was unable to secure a position. In eight years Norman has had no work apart from a period of low-paid, part-time work as the treasurer of a charitable organization. For the past two years, in a booming economy, he has sat at home, doing crossword puzzles, taking the dog for a walk, waiting for a phone call from the agency in town with whom he has placed his c.v. To keep his professional membership he must attend approved courses to update his skills: he resents this imposition.

Norman's self-confidence has declined. With each passing year, his original credentials become more irrelevant. He may never work again. The waste of talent and energy through over-investment in a vocation and under-investment in flexibility is tragic.

In a shifting world, permanent vocations become increasingly problematic. An investment in vocational skills may carry the career actor successfully through early periods of vocational engagement, but unless they are supplemented by updating and further acquisition of interpersonal or business skills, it may be impossible, as Norman found, to maintain career progression.

Sargent was also threatened with the adverse consequences of his own vocationalism and loyalty.

Loving the Job

Sargent left school without any clear sense of direction. But at age 18 he was accepted as a trainee firefighter, and qualified at age 23. He has been a firefighter in the same station ever since (25 years). Occasionally he does unskilled part-time manual work "for doing something different."

Sargent enjoys his work. He likes working out of doors. He is proud of his professionalism. He is multi-skilled as a firefighter. He enjoys the teamwork of firefighting. But he resents recent cuts in staffing and equipment, and the constraints he feels are imposed on his life by the introduction of women firefighters. He also feels his progress has been impeded by an emphasis on exams and qualifications over practical ability. However, he is happy at his level, and has no desire to go up through the ranks. "Two (grades) up you stop fighting fires . . . I [am] happy getting out there and doing it . . . I enjoy being stuck here."

Recently, with the fire service mechanizing, rationalizing, restructuring, and making use of volunteers, Sargent has become increasingly aware of potential pressures on his job. Some older colleagues, but not that much older, have already been laid off.

Sargent seems ill-equipped to embark on anything new. In a service threatened by new, more flexible staffing processes, he is a reluctant but committed trade unionist.

Sargent's job and career are one and the same thing. In Sargent we observe little cumulative adaptation, because he has been in the same role for 25 years, and his only adaptation has been to changes in the role. He is conservative in both career behavior and attitudes, and fearful of ongoing changes in the service. Sargent's career is that of loyal long service. If the service ever stops needing him it is likely that his life will be fractured.

In a service where restructuring continues, and where physical fitness is a key criterion for work performance, there is every chance that eventually Sargent will be forced to give up the career he loves before he wants to. Like Norman, he has invested too much of himself in the vocation, and too little of himself in contingency plans. Sargent is a *true* vocationalist. Since vocations are, by definition, supposed to last forty years, every vocationalist runs these risks.

Making Vocationalism Work

However, many study participants had developed successful careers in a single occupation. It seems that the successful vocationalists are those who have adapted cumulatively by being mobile within their occupation, by consciously seeking new experiences and skills, by adding qualifications as their careers progressed, cultivating occupational networks, and by being willing to accept managerial responsibilities. Typically, these successful vocationalists have moved between employers, acquiring fresh expertise in new areas.

Several apparently successful and satisfied vocationalists in our sample were women who had interrupted their work careers to look after their families, and had returned to the workforce in the occupation for which they had been trained, but with new challenges to face in fresh employment situations. They were apparently the beneficiaries of their own mobility.

Career Success in a Single Occupation

Barbara's (Chapter 7) career in physical therapy has been her only paid employment. Now in her late forties, she has stayed no more than seven years in any one job. She has done extra training all her life, including a specialist program in women's health, a diploma in nursery school supervision, CPR, childhood education, and speech and drama. Her paid and volunteer work have given her service contact with all types of clients, from pre-schoolers to the elderly. She maintains strong contacts with a professional network through which she finds out about work opportunities.

Janice, a professional teacher, quit the school she was working in early in the decade due to a disagreement over an issue of staff discipline. She was well-known as a parent in her children's secondary school, and partly because of this was appointed to a teaching position in it, with some pastoral responsibilities. She worked hard to acquire new skills, for example in school organization, computers, staff administration, and professional development. After a few years she was promoted to take charge of the guidance function, and developed a new set of skills. Approaching retirement, Janice continues to learn at every opportunity.

Quentin's career has been as an air traffic controller. He has worked his way up the ladder from being a cadet. Each job involved more seniority and greater responsibility than the one before. In particular, Quentin learned team and leadership skills. Some years ago, following reorganization of his service, a number of people above him were laid off, and it became clear that the service would become much more open. Quentin responded by studying part-time for a business degree, and, when the opportunity presented itself, applied for a managerial job and got it. When he finishes his degree he may look for a change of direction.

Trust in the Company

In Chapter 5 we described how Lily, an unskilled factory worker, moved from a three-month clerical training program to an accounts clerk position in a supermarket company. Lily's adaptation and integration in the supermarket company was functional to both parties. However, it will not necessarily be functional forever. The experience of other career actors indicates the "down-side" of too strong an investment in one's company. Forces beyond a company's control may force restructuring and the abrupt termination of mutually beneficial career accommodations. Peter (Chapter 1) and Gus (Chapter 3) were able to bring enough learning out of the relationship to turn such situations to their advantage. Not all career actors are so fortunate.

Restructuring a Career

Sam, an accountant, immigrated from overseas, and worked first as an accountant and then as a manager for a company which had sponsored him for his work permit. He found the operation of the company primitive. "There was chaos in the office, half the staff had left, there had been a sort of mutiny." Sam "had to get the whole place organized, I loved that, I used to work till 3 or 4 in the morning sometimes and I wasn't rewarded for that, but it didn't matter to me because I really needed to get it right." He invested socially; team-building and going on social outings with his staff. But after six years the company restructured, Sam's branch was closed, and the company "literally tore up my [employment] contract" and offered him lower status work, which he was not prepared to accept.

A long period of unemployment followed. In his career since his layoff Sam has been downwardly mobile. His current employment is a part-time clerical job. He retains his anger about the way he was treated, and regaled our interviewer with many stories about the corruption of the company. More broadly, he sees big businesses as "a law unto themselves" and believes that "you need to have a trade union to represent you."

Any career actor making Sam's type of investment, year after year, in one company, risks the kind of career hiatus which he experienced. It is not clear why his subsequent career opportunities were so far below expectations for a qualified, experienced person. But one plausible explanation is that in directing all his energies, over six years of intensive work, into the affairs of the company, Sam acquired little learning that was transferable. Perhaps Sam steadily *dis*qualified himself from other work. The greater the investment in company-specific learning, the smaller may be the payoff in the wider economic environment. This problem is potentially greatest, of course, for those who invest not just a few years in a company, as Lily and Sam did, but those who invest their lives.

Restructuring of companies resulting in layoffs creates winners and losers. Sam was a loser. Albert the engineer/barman (Chapter 4) was laid off three times in his earliest career years but was young and resilient enough to shrug off his disappointments and get on with his life. Peter (Chapter 1), the software man, and Gus (Chapter 3), the stevedore, turned restructuring to considerable personal advantage by acting in an entrepreneurial way. (But in both cases many of their colleagues, who were laid off at the same time, lost out). Another interesting case is that of Cedric.

Scaling Down the Career

Cedric had an extensive company career in accounting under successive owners. His roles expanded in the company and included taking over new branches and he "got a real sense of pride" out of running these businesses. But he was fed up with the situation and the time demands and as his wife said, "complaining a lot." His company went through a series of restructurings and eventually he was laid off. He declined two subsequent managerial opportunities, and decided to use his extensive experience and networks to set up on his own. His first business, selling computer consumables, didn't take off but his financial partner did. Cedric learned from that experience, carried on that business, and he and his wife bought another going concern. Together both businesses are now doing well. He carried both his ability and his enjoyment of running the show into his self-employed positions. He had to learn to take on new technical knowledge and more menial roles. "I work long hours but I relax more, and the business attitudes I learned . . . were excellent."

Thus, Cedric has been able to leverage some of the learning acquired in a corporate career to provide a base for his own small businesses. The relevant learning has included not only technical knowledge and skills, but also an understanding of his own motivation, and his networks of business relationships.

Holding on in the Company

As the career advances, many career actors are concerned with "holding on"[8] while at the same time creating something that will outlast them.[9] In many cases there is something about their work, or work group, or the company's culture, which captures their imagination, and with it their careers. These career actors become part of the core of the company,[10] the people who always seem to be there, the repositories of the company's institutional memory, and the guardians of its culture. Sometimes people come to love their companies. In other cases the relationship is a love-hate one, with vigorous championing of the company co-existing uneasily with a recognition of its weaknesses and failings. In all cases, the welfare of both parties becomes increasingly based on the symbiotic relationship between them.

A Life in Court

Elaine applied to work in court administration on a whim after seeing a TV program nearly twenty years ago (see Chapter 4). She has been in court work in her city ever since. Eventually she obtained a senior position. She ensures that she moves to a new department within the court every few years. She takes pride in humanizing and de-bureaucratizing, as far as she can, long-standing systems in her departments. But latterly restructuring of the court system, including staffing reductions, has brought new stresses, and Elaine feels under pressure. In addition, her salary is low and hasn't been increased for six years. To ease financial pressures, she has started telemarketing at home in the evenings, and finds that in a few hours a week she can earn as much as she does from her full-time job. Elaine is 56 now, and still cares deeply about the institution in which she has built her career. Nevertheless, with the pressures on her increasing, she is looking seriously at moving into real estate sales instead.

In twenty years Elaine has made a huge commitment to the institution, and has built up formidable, but institution-specific, expertise. Like many committed employees, for much of the time she "eats, breathes, and sleeps" the court. And while her job appears secure, the court is changing in ways that, for Elaine, reduce the qualities of work life that make it special. For the moment she holds on, but for how long? And how good a preparation for a new job have been her many years of service? Much of her work has been specialized, and court-specific. On the other hand, she has considerable energy and a natural empathy with people. She has spent many years dealing with all sectors of society. And her success at telemarketing has given her confidence in her sales ability. Perhaps the loyal servant, holding on in a rationalizing system, will yet find virtue in discontinuity, and will switch to a totally different line of work.

A number of career actors in our sample had decided, for better or worse, to invest their careers for the foreseeable future (and in some cases, implicitly, until retirement) in specific corporations which they trusted to look after them.

Loyal Company Servants

Kelly had a mobile initial career in which she leveraged language skills and a business diploma to work on cruise ships and travel internationally. In her late thirties, she had had a succession of secretarial jobs in Fotex, a multinational company in the office equipment supply and service industry, to which she had first been contracted as a temporary secretary. She was working as secretary to the technical services manager when a job came up in the department as a customer training representative. The work involved training corporate clients in the use of Fotex equipment. Kelly learned new skills, did the job well, and after a few years was promoted to customer training co-ordinator. She still has customer training responsibilities but is now supervising a team of three. She is 48 and has been with Fotex twelve years.

Kelly enjoys the customer contact. Much of her energy however is focused on outside leisure interests. Following a dissolved marriage and some failed personal relationships, she hopes in due course to find a new long-term relationship. She has never seriously thought of leaving Fotex, or the customer relationships which now mean so much to her.

Piers, aged 54, has trade qualifications as a butcher, but has not worked in the meat industry for 20 years. Sixteen years ago, bored with his repetitive manual job in a brewery, he joined Metalco as a machine operator in a local factory. The job was much more skilled than his previous one, and required exceptional hand-eye coordination. Piers became competent within a few weeks and did the job for eleven years, taking great pride in his expertise. But five years ago he began to have problems with his eyes and was unable to maintain performance. He asked his boss for another job and for two years he supervised others on the machines. But Piers has a strong work ethic, there wasn't enough to do, and he asked for another change. His boss suggested he become a storeman. Piers likes it: "There are no hassles, I do my own thing."

Piers appreciates the way Metalco has looked after him. He is very much a "company man": "I make the employer happy, we look after each other." If for any reason he was unable to continue in his present job, he is confident they'd find him another. He expects to stay with Metalco until he retires.

Kelly and Piers have reached mid-life career adjustment through progressive accommodation with employing companies large enough to have a variety of opportunities available to meet their changing needs, and benevolent enough to look after them in the long-term.

Both have "settled." Both are increasingly dependent on their employers, though of course both would claim that their employers are dependent on them.

Both Kelly and Piers are fortunate that they have chosen companies which have been relatively stable over the years despite fluctuating external conditions. They also benefit from the fact that they are unconstrained by two major forces which complicate many careers: the limitation of specialist qualifications or narrowly focused interests, and the desire to climb the company ladder. As Kelly's and Piers' work careers move towards their conclusions, they value communion above agency, non-work above work. They are undemanding and flexible, and it has not been difficult for their companies to formulate and reformulate appropriate contracts.

Elsewhere in our sample, however, there were career actors, such as Oliver, who showed increasing discomfort as they attempted to adjust the balance between employers' changing structures and requirements, and their own capacities, inclinations, and non-work identities.

Persisting in the Company

Gail, an accounts clerk, is 45. She has been with her current employer for 20 years. In the past ten years she has coped with, and learned from, a location change, a new job description, and new computer systems and software. At one stage she was ambitious and tried to get involved in management. But "when I realized I was getting frustrated because it wasn't happening I pulled back from it, so I don't bother any more." Instead, she puts increasing energy into her outside interests, her home, her cats, her pottery hobby. She dreams of success through her hobby, and talks of becoming self-sufficient by working from home as an accountant. So far, however, she has done nothing to try to implement these dreams.

Stephen is 51. A well-qualified computer expert, he quit his job in a consultancy company thirteen years ago to work full-time for one of its clients, a small engineering company called Hammerford. Since then he has been a self-employed consultant, with Hammerford as his main client. He works from an office at Hammerford and is responsible for the operation and development of the company's computer system. Although he has in the past done some minor software development work outside Hammerford, for the past few years there have been no other contracts. Stephen says his consultant status enables him to earn more money and retain career flexibility. At the same time he acknowledges his dependence on Hammerford. At one stage, when a new boss was determining layoffs at Hammerford, he felt very vulnerable.

Like Kelly and Piers, Gail and Stephen have built long-term alliances with employers, alliances which have lasted into middle age. Despite Gail's dreams of a different life, and Stephen's continuing hope of finding new clients, their real options seem limited, and they may become victims of further restructuring, alterations in their work conditions, or changes in the managerial personnel who currently protect them. Middle-aged people whose skills and experience are employer-specific or over-specialized, and whose energy is perhaps waning, may face major problems if laid off. We conclude that contingency planning is desirable. Even in the most favorable circumstances, trusting all of one's career investments to a single enterprise throughout middle age is risky.

Going for Versatility

Specialization – in occupation or in company – pays premiums for specialist skills, but carries risks for the individual. While conventional career models encourage us to develop as specialists, some people, as we have seen, make a virtue of discontinuity, and develop their careers in an apparently formless way, with few linking specialist themes.

Those who live by specialization may, as we have shown, die by specialization. Those who live by chance and opportunism tend to suffer more hard knocks along the way, but may end up with greater resources for finding their way in a rapidly-changing world, and greater resilience for adapting to misfortune. Two respondents in their fifties were classic examples:

Jack and Jill of All Trades

Ron has been a maintenance mechanic, a barman, and bar manager. He has built his own house, and with his wife has owned and run a small farm, a tavern, an ice cream delivery van, and an ice cream parlor. Seven years ago he acquired his present job as a cigarette delivery van driver, which he acquired through a contact with an acquaintance from a job he had held 15 years previously. His present job is ideal, with regular hours and few demands. Ron uses his savings to take regular overseas holidays, and looks forward to retiring on as much as he needs around the age of 60.

Jean has served in shops, worked a metal press in a factory, been a caretaker, a secretary, a cook, a delicatessen manager, and a food factory supervisor. At different stages she and her husband owned a corner store, a lunch bar, and a candy stall. Not all the jobs and ventures were successful: at one stage they were stuck with an unprofitable lunch bar for several years and eventually sold it at a loss. Now Jean has a steady job as a merchandiser, assisting supermarkets with displays on behalf of suppliers. Through her career run threads of service and an interest in the food businesses.

Ron and Jean have created their own security by always being willing to try something new. Both seem settled, at least for the moment, in their present employment. After turbulent careers, they are in cruise mode. But one has the feeling that if they were for some reason to find themselves out of work, it would not cause the same crisis as it did for Norman and Sam, or as it might do for Kelly or Oliver. Ron and Jean have made many new starts before. They have not invested in qualifications, or occupations, or employers: they have invested in trying what was available, in small-scale enterprise, and in "hard knocks." Now, they are in relatively secure, relatively simple jobs they can handle. If circumstances change, they have the resources to cope.

An instructive contrast with Ron and Jean is the case of Jonathan.

A Failing Investment

Jonathan is 62. His career has been built on the base of his pharmacy qualification. He had ten-years' work as a pharmacist, ten years as a sales representative and manager in a pharmaceutical company, and twenty years owning and managing his own pharmacy.

Until the mid-1980s, Jonathan's prosperity seemed secure. Then a combination of outside forces began to threaten his business. Changes in health policy meant that customers had to pay for previously free drug prescriptions. His store was in a poor area, and in recessionary conditions people tended not to purchase their medicine. Local doctors on whom he had relied left the area. His lease expired and his landlord insisted on a huge rent increase. By 1990 Jonathan had lost three-quarters of his business "through no fault of my own . . . 50 to 55 hours a week and no profit . . . I was barely making wages." He sold the business and got a job as a dispensing pharmacist but left after a "personal incompatibility" with other staff.

Now Jonathan works part-time in an unskilled factory job offered to him by a neighbor. He has been there a year, but is beginning to think of retiring.

Jonathan's recent career indicates the perils of investment in a single occupation and of self-employment as a career strategy. Jonathan blames external forces such as the government, the locality, and his landlord for his failure. But perhaps he failed to watch for warning signs, and did not acquire the managerial and business skills which his career required. Perhaps, in his last pharmacist job, his interpersonal skills were found wanting. Unable to continue in the occupation and industry in which he had built his career, he found his options limited, albeit late in his career when it mattered less. Despite the business failure, Jonathan has been fortunate, for his hard work over a long career has apparently enabled him to acquire sufficient financial capital to enjoy a comfortable retirement.

Dealing with Adversity

The disruption of informed direction or seasoned engagment in a work career can come, as we have seen, from changes in family circumstances (Chapter 5), or from occupational obsolescence (Norman the accountant) or employer restructuring (Sam the accountant). But it may also come from personal circumstance and tragedy. None of us knows when illness or accident may enforce radical change on our career. In the course of their lives, a number of our sample have had to deal with major adversities, such as personal injury or disability, and relationship break-ups that altered personal psyches and family responsibilities. Some were trapped in a difficult situation while others battled their way out of one. All have shown tenacity and courage in drawing on their own and, at times, others' resources, to endure and to move forward.

Toughing it Out

Cliff comes from a building family. He followed the family line by starting as an apprentice builder. Eventually he had left a secure local authority job to work with his architect brother-in-law. But he injured his back and was off work for 12 months. He still has no feeling in the lower half of one leg. As a result Cliff has been able to do only small jobs with his builder brother. He has fears of ending up in a wheelchair but is generally philosophical, living with the constraints of his injury in the ups and downs of self employment: "You have to take the good with the bad . . . just tough it out."

Bill is striving to emerge from a history of temporary unskilled labor, and more significantly the effects of a major road accident which put him out of the community for a year. He has constant pain in his legs and cannot do sustained physical work. Although he is currently unemployed, Bill is trying to use his contacts and fragmented experience in the music industry to develop a way for himself. Significantly his wife – the "best thing" to happen to Bill in the past ten years – has successfully reclaimed family land and Bill has a broad vision of developing a tourist venture on this land and "providing a future for my children."

Both Cliff and Bill had begun their careers, made some headway, and acquired some skills when disaster struck. Further out on the margins of the workforce, are those whose misfortune has come much earlier, those who seem handicapped by circumstances of class, race, urban or rural background; who are alienated from, and by, the workaday world of commerce and employment. In such a context, the early notions of "career" with its cosy assumptions of meaning and permanence, and even the later definitons of "career" focused on continuously developing sequences of jobs, seem out of place. Yet in this unpromising ground we may still find inspiring examples of the human transformations that can take place when individuals take their destiny into their own hands, and focus, through ongoing adversity, on doing something worthwhile.

Battling Adversity

Elisabeth comes from a disadvantaged background of poverty, belonging to an ethnic minority, and virtually no education. She was brought up to believe that she was "dumb" and that she had nothing to contribute. She was sent to the city early in adolescence where an agency placed her in domestic service with a family. She was paid but the employer had control of her bank book. This disempowered employment situation coupled with her illiteracy made even simple living tasks difficult. She met her husband during this period. They eventually moved to another country, experiencing blatant racism while trying to get rental accommodation. Elisabeth wanted to work with old people and summoned up the courage to go on a course, "but the words were very big and I didn't understand." She found literacy classes in her local community. It took four weeks before she dared to go, but once she was there the classes proved to be a turning point. Her tutors and fellow-students proved to be great mutual support and many became friends. Over six years of night classes she has learned to read and write; this has had a huge impact on her confidence and her self-knowlege of her ability to learn. She has been to other courses, such as sewing and screen printing, all of which may help her to get more fulfilling work. She has published a book of her experiences growing up. Her driver's licence has given her mobility. Elisabeth has shown great courage in overcoming her illiteracy and battling adverse conditions: racism, her own diabetes, coping with a child with a chronic illness, and her husband who is often unemployed in the winter. Her advice to others is an understatement of the courage and strength that she has shown: "Once you decide you are going to do something, don't let things stand in your way, look ahead."

Elisabeth's life provides an inspirational role model of courage, strength and perseverance. Her life demonstrates the impact of coming from a disadvantaged position and yet battling to overcome adversity. Her learning and confidence have grown with each new challenge and in turn she has slowly increased the choices within which she enacts her life.

As is the case for so many of the sample, Elisabeth's career has not followed the orderly patterns suggested by traditional theorists such as Levinson and Super.[11] Elisabeth needed the opportunity for release from a debilitating period in adolescence and early adulthood in which conventional career development was not possible. Her emancipation occurred long after she took on family responsibilities. In her own way, Elisabeth demonstrated the common career assertiveness among women in middle adulthood.[12]

Creating a Calmer Lifestyle

As seasoned career actors move towards the end of their careers, they are able to focus greater attention on their lifestyle – on physical and mental health, homes, families, and leisure interests. More than previously, lifestyle may be a matter of choice, something to be deliberately enacted into career decisions rather than passively hoped for as a career outcome. The "empty nest" after the departure of children, and in some cases continuing financial prosperity, reduce immediate pressures. Those in stable jobs "work smarter" to reduce job stress. Possibilities increase, the attractiveness of creating an enduring way of life which will satisfy the "whole person" grows. Increasingly, lifestyle becomes an end, and work merely the means. Individuals become less concerned with "career success," and seek ways to "look after themselves" in their career choices.

Consider the following individuals, all in their late forties or early fifties:

Adjusting Work to Develop Lifestyle

Ron and Jean (Chapter 6), have both recognized the extra efforts and stresses of the self-employment which had been so prevalent in their earlier careers, and have wound down into steady jobs with regular hours that leave them with free time. Neither has any intention of returning to self-employment.

Dan (Chapter 3) cashed in the career and financial capital represented by his partnership in a merchant bank, and used the money to purchase property. As a part-time landlord he is able to give priority to his family and his leisure interests.

Anne is an office worker who has always put home and family ahead of career, chiefly by ensuring that her workplace was close to home and by avoiding promotion and responsibility. Now she is forced by her husband's unemployment to work longer hours than she would like, but she constantly looks for ways in which she can reduce her work commitment while continuing to do a good job.

Cedric gave up a high-stress corporate role to run two small businesses in the office supplies industry. His income is reduced, but he sees opportunities to "wind down" his work hours, "be more flexible," "work on a part-time basis," and spend "more time with my children."

Jennie has for many years worked long hours, for low wages in "caring" positions looking after intellectually disabled people. But she has recently been physically threatened, and feels "you can't go on forever." She has good networks, and is exploring ways of changing employment, getting a more equitable wage, and building a nest-egg for retirement.

Looking to Retirement

As careers wind down, families become independent and retirement becomes a focus. Career actors begin to think about life after work. Some of our older participants had firm plans for retirement. The idea seemed to be welcomed by most, though some were worried about not having enough money. Most looked forward to part-time work, voluntary service, hobbies, or further education. Although some had plans which would enable them to utilize further the skills and knowledge accumulated during their working careers, for the most part participants looked forward to being able to undertake activities which were not possible in conjunction with the demands of their current employment. Two women hoped they would be able to continue to go to the gym. A man wanted to go bowling "three times a day." Another hoped to go on safari in Africa. Several wanted to travel. There was little sense, in these responses, of life being over in retirement.

A particularly strong response to the question of retirement came from Janice, aged 56, the career schoolteacher and counselor introduced earlier in this chapter. She expresses a somewhat radical view of the education system:

I want to retire at 60, there are a lot of other things I want to do. I want to move out of the city, although my husband and I don't necessarily agree on this. I want some time to do things for myself. I want more education, I am longing to do a project on the way the school system tends to support the status quo. I want to spend time fighting against what's happening, against the emerging class system that we've got. Another idea that I've got has to do with the absurdities of school, in terms of education schools are a ridiculous concept. I'd like to write something about that. I'd like to work in a shop. I'd love to work in an antique shop. I want to get fit again. I'll go to Tai Chi.

Janice clearly plans to use her career experience, in the form of knowledge about the education system and attitudes to it, in retirement. She sees retirement as a liberating force which will enable her to express her passion about education in a new form with broader objectives. At the same time, she looks forward to new activities. For Janice, retirement is not about severing her connections with her work experience. Rather, it is about sourcing further "fresh energy" to embark on a new cycle of career activity.

We close this chapter, fittingly, with the story of the only already retired member of our sample, who in his ongoing career behavior shows, as well as anyone, the utilization of past skills, the support of personal networks, the energy of new pursuits, and the enactment of individual choice which we believe will become the hallmarks of many future careers.

Starting Over

Bert retired from a manual work career six years ago, at age 60, to look after his invalid wife. He had enough money saved for a comfortable but modest lifestyle. When his wife died three years later, he fulfilled a long-term ambition by building his own motor home, using skills acquired in a lifetime of jobs working with machinery. He then spent several months touring. At the end of the tour he sold the motor home and rented a small apartment in a city far from the locality where he had spent his life. He was briefly involved in a business selling candy, but gave it up due to tax complications.

One day his niece invited him to visit her square dancing club. He found he enjoyed square dancing. He joined the club and took up dancing as a regular pastime. He now travels widely in the area, visiting other clubs. At one square dance, an acquaintance offered him a part-time job driving children to and from school by taxi. He obtained his taxi license and continues to work in the job. The money helps, and the work fills in his day nicely. But when asked about the future, Bert talks not about his taxi, but about his aspirations as a square dancer.

Both Janice and Bert have lived most of their careers in an earlier era of the Industrial State. However, both their careers suggest that creative combining of "Fresh Energy," "Informed Direction," and "Seasoned Engagement" can continue to open up fresh career opportunities in the New Economy. We will face that suggestion directly in the next chapter.

Notes

1. Super, D.E. *The Psychology of Careers*. New York: Harper & Row, 1957; Super, D.E. A life-span, life-space approach to career development. In D. Brown and L. Brooks (eds.) *Career Choice and Development*. San Francisco: Jossey-Bass, 1990, pp. 197–261.

2. Super, D.E. Towards a comprehensive theory of career development. In D.H. Montross and C.J. Shinkman (eds.) *Career Development: Theory and Practice*. Springfield, IL: Charles C. Thomas, 1992, p. 44.

3. Erikson, E.H. *Childhood and Society* (2nd ed.). New York: Norton, 1963.

4. Arthur, M.B. and Kram, K.E. Reciprocity at work: the separate, yet inseparable possibilities for individual and organizational development. In M.B. Arthur, D.T. Hall and B.S. Lawrence (eds.) *Handbook of Career Theory*. Cambridge: Cambridge University Press, 1989, pp. 292–312.

5. Super, D.E. (1992). op. cit. (2), p. 44.

6. Goffee, R. and Scase, R. (1992). Organizational change and the corporate career: the restructuring of managers' aspirations. *Human Relations*, 45: 363–85.

7. Super (1992), op. cit. (2), p. 44.

8. Super (1957), op. cit. (1).

9. Levinson, D.J., Darrow, C.N., Klein, E.B., Levinson, M.H. and McKee, B. *The Seasons of a Man's Life*. New York: Knopf, 1978.

10. Handy, C. *The Age of Unreason*. Boston: Harvard University Press, 1989.

11. Super (1957), op cit. (1); Levinson et al., op cit. (9).

12. Gallos, J. Exploring women's development: implications for career theory, practice, and research. In Arthur, Hall and Lawrence, op. cit. (4).

7 Turning Career Competencies into Career Capital

A Life of Service

Barbara qualified as a physical therapist 25 years ago, when she was in her early twenties. Her early career included several hospital jobs in physical therapy (P.T.) and five years of travel away from home. During these early years Barbara made a number of "P.T. friends" to whom she would remain close. By the time she returned to her home city she was married. She continued full-time in hospital physical therapy work, then became pregnant with the first of her three children.

Barbara continued to work part-time during her children's pre-school years. She lived close to the hospital, and made sure that her work was confined to week-ends, when her husband could look after the children. Her career was important to her, providing her with a role other than "mother" and giving stimulation, professional identity, and a sense of service. During this time Barbara also did play center supervisory training and became an assistant supervisor.

Nine years ago Barbara's husband was offered a better job in another city and the family moved. Now that her children were all at school, Barbara could be more flexible in the hours she worked. Through a P.T. friend she heard about a job in a local maternity hospital, working with pregnant women. Barbara took the job, which involved helping women to prepare for childbirth. She held it for seven years. She found the work of assisting pregnant women very worthwhile from the point of view of supportive service: "Often we were the people the women spoke to that nobody else had time for." She acquired teaching skills and completed a postgraduate diploma in women's health.

Eighteen months after completing the postgraduate course, Barbara left maternity work. She felt that it had become routine, she was bothered by political struggles in the hospital, and expectations of her to work longer hours were interfering with her family responsibilities. At that stage Barbara contemplated a major career change. She applied for a job as a receptionist and was rejected as being over-qualified. She applied for nursing training and found that because of her qualifications she could be fast-tracked to complete the program in half the time. But after discussing the opportunity with her husband and some therapy friends, Barbara decided to stick with what she knew.

Coincidentally, she heard through a contact about a physical therapy vacancy in a rest home for elderly people. She was interviewed and got the job, which she has now held for a year. She gains great enjoyment – "I love every day" – and a sense of contribution from her work with the elderly: "I think the elderly have taught me much more than I thought was possible just by being with them . . . I guess they taught me wisdom comes with age . . . that every one is unique and like a group of any age, primary school children or a class of pregnant women, they are as diverse as we are . . . The kinds of people they have been and the contribution they have made . . . it's been quite a humbling experience . . . ." For the future, she plans to continue in her therapy work for another ten or fifteen years, perhaps with the elderly, perhaps not.

What are the key features of Barbara's unfolding career? First, she has, since her pregnancy with her first child, composed it to be complementary to her role as a wife and mother. Job changes and work schedules have depended on accommodating both work and home roles. Secondly, it is clearly an occupational career: while Barbara has occasionally toyed with ideas of moving into other types of work, in the end she has always remained true to her career roots. Thirdly, a "career anchor"[1] of social service runs through everything that Barbara does, including her activities in pre-school education and other voluneer roles. Fourthly, in relation to the "agency-communion" dimension which we outlined in Chapter 3, it has been a career of almost pure communion, particularly in respect of Barbara's relationships with clients. Her important reciprocal exchanges have been with her client groups, for example pregnant women and elderly people. Finally, one cannot help but notice the importance to Barbara of her "P.T. friends," the lifelong network of professional contacts who recur through her story, and who draw attention to job opportunities, provide and receive counsel, and generally help Barbara to manage her career.

Developing Career Competencies

Barbara's career illustrates the concept of "career competencies," the acquisition of such competencies by the career actor, and their accumulation over time.

As Barbara enacts her career, she learns. However, her learning changes in emphasis and direction. Her initial competencies at work were acquired through her upbringing, school experience, and training as a therapist. As Barbara recognizes, that training has become out-of-date. However, her therapy experiences in leading hospitals have facilitated a more confident and versatile practitioner. New client groups and types of work have affirmed Barbara's occupational identity and have provided her with additional skills. Home-based and work experiences appear to have contributed to and complemented each other. At one stage, for example, her personal experience of pregnancy and childbirth powerfully influenced her choice of jobs within the maternity hospital. Courses and qualifications formalized and accredited important learning. At the same time, as she specialized, her lack of practice in some areas – for example intensive care – slipped from Barbara's current repertoire.

One way to organize and understand Barbara's career competencies is to consider them as complementary to an employing company's "core competencies." These competencies may be reliably mapped in terms of three overlapping arenas: *company culture, know-how*, and *networks*.[2] Briefly, culture embodies the values and beliefs behind the company's mission and strategic purpose; know-how involves the company's accumulated skills and understanding of its present circumstances; and networks represent the relationships through which a company relates to suppliers, customers, alliance partners, and other participants in the economic marketplace.[3] A company may compete by emphasizing any one of these three competency types, but is more likely to do so through some distinctive combination of all three.

The career complements to the firm's developing competencies may be termed *knowing-why, knowing-how*, and *knowing-whom*.[4] Knowing-why competencies are concerned with issues of personal identity and meaning, and are complementary to the mission and culture of employing companies, as well as to the particular company roles that career actors occupy. These knowing-why competencies provide the motivational energy on which the individual's efforts in the company are based. Knowing-how competencies encompass the skills and understanding people accumulate through their work and education. These knowing-how skills frequently develop through, and become embedded in, the technical and managerial "know-how" of employing companies. Knowing-whom competencies are not just abilities to relate to others and to develop contacts, but also the networks of people, and reputation with other people, which are built up as the career progresses. These knowing-whom competencies connect with, change, and are changed by, the company-specific networks in which the career actor participates.

The application of the career competencies frame of reference to Barbara's career may be illustrated by sample quotes from her interview transcript.

Barbara's knowing-why gets its stability from her deeply-rooted desire to serve, her satisfying exchange with clients, and her strong identification with her professional practice of physical therapy. It gets its dynamic from her need for novelty, stimulation, and challenge, and from the ever-changing requirements of her family role. For example:

Working part-time, with children at home: I used to walk through the hospital thinking, "I'm Barbara Smith, physical therapist, not mother of screaming children" . . . it also gave me a little bit of financial independence . . . I also enjoyed the stimulation, I liked helping a variety of conditions and people . . . I felt I had a profession I didn't want to lose touch with.

Leaving the maternity hospital: After seven years and a lot of changes in the health system I was ready for a change. I think it had become a bit of the sameness, I had finished the postgraduate course about a year before. There was a lot more politics going on as far as nurses and midwives within the hospital . . . conditions were not as good as they had originally been. So I was looking for a change, I was just stale and also I was having to do a lot of Saturday morning classes and evening classes and things that were beginning to encroach upon family life in a way that I felt I didn't want to happen.

Knowing-how is embodied in Barbara's initial training, her accumulating professional practice, her specialist experience within that practice, the learning embodied within her additional qualifications, and the growing wisdom she acquires through her non-work roles. For example:

The maternity hospital job: There was a steep learning curve, because I had gone into the women's health field. I hadn't done a lot apart from the obligatory pre-natal classes that everybody did and nobody really enjoyed . . . [It was] a terrific learning curve. I treated women of all ages with leaky bladders and all sorts of gynaecological conditions and that was a very privileged position.

Learning off the job: One of the [best] things that springs to mind was going on a personal growth course and leadership course with my husband. It taught me to take risks and gave me the opportunity to grow personally and extend my skills of leadership, within a personal and professional capacity.

Knowing-whom embraces a range of contacts and networks which Barbara has developed over the years, most obviously the "P.T. friends," but also other work contacts as well as her family, neighbors, volunteer activity associates, and of course her clients. For example:

Getting the maternity hospital job: A P.T. friend of mine . . . [was called] about a job at a maternity hospital, and at that time she had very tiny babies and was stacking shelves in the supermarket, so she rang me and said, "I can't do it, do you want to apply?" So I got the job by word of mouth.

Getting a new job: One of the physical therapists I had worked with and done the course with . . . had been away overseas and came back and was looking for work and I had got her into Eastern Maternity Hospital because of the timing, and then she moved back to Cypresses Rest Home, all word of mouth. She was being put upon to do a bit more, she wanted to do 20 hours but was expected to do 30, it was too stressful, so she moved from Cypresses Rest Home after a year to work for her husband. She knew I was looking for a change, and I went out for an interview.

What Distinguishes Career Competencies?

Career competencies are personal competencies which have the potential to become competencies of the employing institution. They are put temporarily at the employer's disposal, and become part of the reciprocal exchange between the two parties. However, the benefits from career competencies often outlast the employment relationship, for example when a worker passes on values or skills to others, institutionalizes them in company procedures or culture, or brokers a new business relationship for the company from among his or her own contacts. It is likely that some of Barbara's expertise developed in the maternity hospital remains there as a residue of practices, procedures, and perhaps attitudes among her former colleagues and clients. But the same expertise has also been retained by Barbara to be used in her new employment. There it becomes a moving base on to which new competencies are grafted, for example, her new facility with the elderly and the wisdom she acquires from them.

It is instructive to compare the notion of "career competencies" with the more widely-known idea of "managerial competencies."[5] Studies of managerial competencies are based on concepts of a company's competency needs and corresponding individual managerial skills. They are typically framed in conventional, work-based schema of "technical competencies," "interpersonal competencies," and "conceptual" or "strategic competencies," and relate directly to the job to be performed. In contrast, the "career" spans wider social roles, occupies a much longer time-frame than the "job," and provides a more complex framework for conceptualizing competencies and their accumulation.

Companies often attempt to specify competencies in terms of "bodies of knowledge" or "required skills." For example, "What are the competencies we require to meet our strategic objectives? What are the competencies we already possess? What is the gap? What new human resources do we need to acquire or develop in order to close the gap?" Thus, action is defined and limited by the institution's own objectives. While some attention is paid to the knowing-how competencies of employees, the knowing-why and knowing-whom are largely neglected, as are the wider life arenas in which competencies develop. In addition, the possibility is ignored of employees bringing unanticipated competencies to the company which may stimulate unplanned but desirable developments.

Paying attention to career competencies suggests new possibilities for both career actors and employing companies. Career actors may choose to "decouple" their identities and development from company settings, and may integrate their lives around their own, self-defined learning.[6] Companies may opportunistically leverage new learning from their employees, gaining novel direction rather than being tied to any formal plan. In these scenarios "career planning" is not about investigating how individual careers can be directed to enhance company objectives, but rather about gathering individuals' reflections on their developing careers and seeing how these can be incorporated into company learning and can lead to new business opportunities.

From Career Competencies to Career Capital

Career competencies, earned through education, work, and life experience, accumulate into what we will call *career capital*. Career capital may gather further value or lose it, or be traded for fresh capital. For example, knowing-how higher education qualifications obtained when young (such as Barbara's physical therapy certification) may provide the demonstration of base expertise which enables the graduate to find a first job. The job may provide further inspiration (knowing-why), expertise (knowing-how) or network connections (knowing-whom) which a second employer may value. Moving from opportunity to opportunity, the career actor simultaneously discharges work responsibilities, adapts to new situations, and builds additional career capital. In the process, original qualifications and past experiences may recede into the background, and cease to have more than symbolic value. Over time, skills and networks may become obsolete and their direct contribution to career capital may decline. But they may also be used to exchange on-the-job performance for the chance to build new career capital with a better prognosis of future value.

In other cases, career actors often find that there are few opportunities to invest career capital. Perhaps the most publicized cases involve people who presumed their jobs were secure and only realized their circumstances under the stress of unanticipated job loss.[7] Such people may, out of a false sense of security, have simply neglected to invest in new career competencies, or they may have invested in company-specific, non-transferable skills. However, it is not only laid-off workers who may find that unemployment is a problem, or that the market for their specific competencies is limited. Many people whose competencies were developed in idiosyncratic ways or non-work roles – such as the managerial skills of women running their families and homes – are undervalued. Marshall tells powerful but depressing stories about women managers who found that their competencies were not appreciated by their employing companies and could not be developed in those settings.[8]

As we have shown in Chapter 6, career capital accumulations may occasionally pay off through secure, enjoyable, long-term employment in a benevolent company. But they may also deteriorate in value, particularly if no new accumulation takes place. In the New Economy, the unfolding of career experiences and the career capital that one builds from them are vital. As in the world of financial capital, successful strategies of the past carry no guarantees for the future. People relying on a particular trade, degree, or professional certification, or on a company promising lifetime employment, may see their stock of career capital much diminished unless they take continuous steps to sustain it.

A further correspondence in the analogy of financial and career capital may be noted: the parallel between financial portfolios and "portfolio careers."[9] As financial wisdom counsels us to spread our risks by having a portfolio of diverse shares and bonds, so modern career theory urges us to think laterally in building career capital. Barbara's case provides an interesting example. Over her long career and extensive competency accumulation in physical therapy, she has acquired a range of wider competencies in service orientation, in client relationships, in dealing with vulnerable groups, in networking, in being alive to new opportunities. One feels that even if the practice of her occupation were banned tomorrow, she would be so versatile that she could continue in some other role in her portfolio, and make a difference almost without breaking stride.

However, the analogy between career capital and financial capital can be taken too far. People may be neither rational nor goal-directed in their accumulation of career capital. To place a dollar value on people's career experience is to objectify something which has major subjective elements. Individuals like Barbara whose career behavior is largely an expression of non-economic core values, and whose orientation is to communion rather than agency, acquire career capital almost inadvertently, not as a planned return from a calculative strategy, but as a values-driven outcome of their inner selves. Even the more agentic types, like Peter (Chapter 1) appear driven in their career behavior more by a generalized desire to develop themselves than by a calculated assessment of long-term rewards.

Cycles of Career Capital Accumulation

How do people engage in the accumulation of career competencies? In order to understand this, we need to focus on careers at a more micro-level. We need to see how career actors assemble the specific experiences they have gained through their projects and jobs into competencies which endure and provide a continuing source of capital accumulation.

In Chapters 4 to 6 we outlined a conventional "stage" model of careers to indicate patterns of career development through successive phases of exploring, advancing, and maintaining/completing. We used the model as a means of grouping and understanding data about three groups of actors, mainly at particular ages and stages of career. However, as we observed in Chapter 3, the concept of stage can be applied to more micro-level forms of career behavior, for example, to a job or a project.

In Barbara's case, for example, we can see her seven-year job in the maternity hospital as a cycle of exploring, advancing, and finally concluding. The initial "buzz" which Barbara got from early sessions with pregnant women gave way to a concern about becoming a professional expert on women's health through her postgraduate program of study. Eventually, Barbara tired of her role at work, and came to feel stale, disillusioned by hospital politics, and concerned to preserve her "family time." She moved into a new cycle, based in the rest home. A job may be seen as a cycle within a career cycle. Within the job cycle, a single project or client or physical therapy session may be a smaller cycle again. Thus, broad career patterns are built from myriad fragments of work experience assembling themselves progressively into longer and wider cycles.[10]

Significant examples of boundaryless career behavior are found in industries such as film-making and scientific research which define themselves on a project-to-project basis in terms of financing, final product, etc. For the purpose of the industry contribution, such projects are collaborative, yet each project is also a personal career project for the individuals involved. In such cases, the "one-time" nature of the product powerfully dictates that it is the projects rather than the jobs that provide the most useful episodes into which to divide, and through which to analyse, careers.[11]

Thinking about careers as the enactment of projects is another way of turning Industrial State thinking on its head. In their work on "the personal projects enterprise strategy," for example, Freeman and Gilbert see enterprise being created in corporations by means of people passing through on their way to other projects, quite likely in other corporations. "Corporations," they say, "can be thought of as sets of agreements between the members to achieve their projects."[12] The point has been popularized by management consultant Tom Peters who sees work returning to the project-based craft tradition that preceded the factory system on which the era of the Industrial State was built. Instead, he proposes a "what-can-I-learn-next" micro-project approach unfolding within a macro-career context.[13] This is reminiscent of Weick's view (Chapter 3) of frequent, intense periods of personal development occurring "with more intensity in smaller gatherings."[14]

Our participants did not generally talk directly about projects, nor were they particularly responsive when we asked about projects. Perhaps this was because of our own job-to-job framing of questions about the career story, and the narrow common meaning of what a "project" entails. But many participants talked about projects – in the sense of cyclic episodes involving completion and learning – without using the word. The pattern is clearly evident in the jobs making up Barbara's career. Other examples illustrate successive projects occurring within the same job. For example, farmer Alex was involved in long-term experimentation with "sabbatical fallow" land usage – a project which would take many years to complete. Court registrar Elaine's (Chapter 6) talk about court reform was in essence a description of a set of self-initiated projects into which she enlisted the help of project collaborators. Personal assistant Anne (Chapter 6) would see a new computer software package as essentially a project to be mastered.

The analogy between jobs and projects, however, emerges more powerfully in retrospective descriptions. The way people looked back on the jobs they had performed, the fact that most inter-company job moves were voluntary, and the descriptions of how those moves came about, combined to convey a composite image. It was an image of a project or cycle reaching a natural conclusion, and of both parties to the employment contract having been served. We turn next to consider *how* each of the parties was served.

Cycles and Reciprocal Benefits

In boundaryless careers, which represent the experience of most of our participants, career competencies accumulate through reciprocal benefits (Chapter 1) exchanged between career actor and employing institution. We emphasize here that competencies exchanged reciprocally may outlast the relationship which initiated them. A departing employee's career competencies are available for use in his or her subsequent jobs, but they may also be retained in the ongoing culture, know-how, or networks of the company which the employee has left.

The nature of knowledge accumulation can be revealed in underlying patterns of reciprocal exchange. We explored this by asking people a matching pair of questions for each job they reported: "What did you get [from the job]?" and "What did you give [to the job]?" In evaluating these benefits, we must bear in mind a limitation in our data. It is easier for individuals to be specific about what they receive from the job than about what they give. Employees contribute effort, expertise, etc., to the employer, but the assessment of the value received must come from the employer. Even then, it is difficult to measure, since some of the contributions to company culture, know-how and networks may be inadequately captured in performance appraisal systems or other repositories of "company memory."

A principal distinction emerged in our data between "bounded" and "boundaryless" benefits. By a *bounded* benefit we mean one that lasts only as long as the person continues in the job, such as money or job satisfaction received by the career actor, or dependability of work performance given to the employer. By a *boundaryless* benefit we mean one that persists after the person has left the job, such as the job experience or coaching received and retained by the career actor, or the new office procedures or customers retained by the employer. A given set of reciprocal benefits can therefore involve possibilities based on "What did you get?" versus "What did you give?" set against "bounded" versus "boundaryless" benefits received by each party.

Where the actor both gets and gives bounded benefits, the transaction is a "here-and-now" contract whose benefits are confined to the present relationship and imply no long-term benefits beyond that relationship for either the employee's career or the company's future operation. Take the case of Barry, introduced in Chapter 4:

> Interviewer: What did you get from that job?
> Barry: A weekly pay packet. I suppose I got some experience of working in the food trade in different areas.
> Interviewer: What did you give to that job?
> Barry: I suppose I gave myself to the job, I did the job to the best of my ability.

Barry's initial answer to "What did you get?" – "A weekly pay packet" – is a bounded benefit. On the other hand, "experience of working in the food industry" is boundaryless, since it is implicitly transferable beyond the immediate employment situation. On the other hand, Barry's entire answer to "What did you give?" is bounded by the situation.

In contrast, there is Catherine (Chapter 2):

> Interviewier: What did you get from that job?
> Catherine (the young marketing professional, Chapter 2): I learned a lot more about marketing and business management, sort of like being a student again . . . I learned a lot of confidence and maturity in myself because I was suddenly thrown into a responsible position.
> Interviewier: What did you give to that job?
> Catherine: A lot of very practical things, student education, developed the library . . . I gave the students a lot of help, one-on-one . . . I gave the lecturers a lot of ideas . . . They said I'd brought a breath of fresh air to the department . . . I think because I'd done the promotional stuff, when I left they did appoint a marketing manager, which is good, and they started ads on TV.

Catherine's view is boundaryless, in respect of both her own career and the institution. As she does her job, she develops knowing-how skills and knowing-why self-assurance which benefit her career. Simultaneously, the institution develops new arrangements which are not dependent on Catherine in the long-term and will outlast her departure. Catherine even talks specifically about events which took place in the institution after she left, which she attributes to her efforts while there.

Benefits for the Company

The main types of bounded benefits mentioned by participants for their companies fell into five main categories. Most frequent was committed work performance, where people said something about being particularly involved in the job, or being dedicated, or giving their best effort. Second was basic work performance, such as putting in the required time or doing the work as expected. Third was the application of personal skills, knowledge, or experience. Fourth was extended work performance, where people offered something more than a statement of work commitment, for example highlighting their level of energy, or claiming to give their "souls" to the job. Finally, to a lesser degree, were explicit claims to doing things differently, through the jobholder's own methods, project management, or organizing abilities.

Table 7.1 *Incidence of bounded and boundaryless benefits, given by career actors to their jobs*

	Number of mentions of benefit
Bounded benefits	
Committed work performance	69
Basic work performance	35
Applying personal skills or experience	29
Extended work performance	26
Doing things differently	8
Total	167
Boundaryless benefits	
Bringing learning to others	10
Establishing new systems	9
"Moving the bottom line"	6
Contributing to teamwork	6
Restructuring and changing	5
Introducing new vision	2
Total	38

The main types of boundaryless benefits reported for companies fell into the following six categories. Most frequently mentioned was bringing learning to others through training or teaching. Second was establishing new systems, such as new office or computer processes, or new operational arrangements, which persisted beyond the employment period. The next most frequent was a claim to "move the bottom line" through direct contributions to a company's profitability, business, or customer base, or its strategic positioning. Fourth was contributing to teamwork, and having an enduring influence on the other team members. Fifth was contributing to specific restructuring or change efforts. Finally, there was influencing the company's or its members' vision of the work or mission undertaken.

Both sets of reported bounded and boundaryless benefits are summarized in Table 7.1

Thus, out of 205 benefits which career actors claimed to have given to their jobs, 167, or 81 percent, were restricted to the current employment relationship. Most of these were of the kind described earlier for Barry: putting in required time, being dependable, and doing one's best.

In contrast, 38, or 19 percent, of the benefits identified were seen as benefits that would prevail beyond the person's employment period. For example:

I computerised a few things for them. Everything was in its infancy, but I set up a couple of spreadsheets for them which I think they still use today. (Sam)

I actually saved them a lot of money. They had a lot of ingredients [which] were a lot more expensive than other ingredients that were just as good. It was quite easy to save them hundreds of thousands of dollars just by changing one ingredient in their recipe. (Susan)

I think I contributed a fresh way of doing things. For example I thought the school should be "de-streamed" . . . I was able to bring in ideas from elsewhere, I was able to give ideas from my own children's school. (Janice)

Around half of the reports of giving boundaryless benefits came from the first two (managerial and professional) occupational groups in our sample; the others were distributed evenly across the remaining occupational groups. It is predictable that these first two groups would be both more conscious of, and more likely to articulate, the company's greater benefits. However, it is also predictable that this group would be more verbal about their contributions than people from the other occupational groups. Our data, based on individual perceptions, do not allow for a full picture of boundaryless company benefits to emerge. However, the data do provide an interesting contrast to people's perceptions of what they got in return for what they gave.

Benefits for the Person

Participants' reports of bounded benefits to themselves from their jobs fell into six categories. The most frequently mentioned benefits involved specific work satisfaction, such as finding challenge, interest or responsibility in the work performed. Next came money, or the opportunity to make a living. A third group of benefits involved enjoyment at work, including having fun, free time, relaxation or travel opportunities. A fourth group covered social life, including making friends, and enjoying social interactions. Next came safety and support in the work environment. Finally came autonomy, or a sense of freedom or choice in the work performed.

Participants' reports of the boundaryless benefits to themselves from their jobs also fell into six categories. Most frequently mentioned by a large margin was the learning of new skills and knowledge, including new ways of working or developing one's talents. Second, enhanced personal networks, getting to know new people or to know people better, and gaining greater reputation. Third, self-assurance,

Table 7.2 *Incidence of bounded and boundaryless benefits, received by career actors from their jobs*

	Number of mentions of benefit
Bounded benefits	
Specific work satisfactions	47
Money	29
Enjoyment	20
Social life	12
Safety and support	7
Autonomy	3
Total	118
Boundaryless benefits	
Skills and knowledge	89
Enhanced networks	14
Self-assurance	9
Personal growth	9
Broader viewpoint	9
Communication skills	5
Total	135

such as a boost in self-confidence or a greater sense of control over one's destiny stemming from the job experience. Fourth, personal growth, such as meeting new developmental challenges or gaining deeper self-knowledge. Fifth, a broadening of viewpoint, for example seeing things in a new or more professional perspective. Sixth, communication skills, both written and verbal varieties, including skills in providing training.

The benefits which participants reported in answer to the question, "What did you get [from the job]?" are summarized in Table 7.2.

Thus, out of 253 benefits which participants reported receiving from jobs, 118 (47%) were bounded and 135 (53%) were boundaryless. Interestingly, the reports of bounded benefits correspond closely to traditional ideas about "job satisfaction" with "lower order needs" (money, enjoyment, social life, and safety and support) somewhat outnumbering "higher order needs" (specific work satisfactions and autonomy).[15] However, the fact that more than half of the reported benefits were boundaryless – that is transferable to another company – points to substantial limitations of traditional job satisfaction approaches to the study of work.

It is important to observe that participants reported giving bounded benefits more than five times as often as they reported giving boundaryless benefits. In contrast, they reported receiving

boundaryless benefits more often than bounded benefits. These
boundaryless benefits, retained after a person leaves the job, provide a
key to understanding career competency accumulation.

Benefits in Knowing-How

Boundaryless benefits from specific jobs enhance overall career
competencies, whereas bounded benefits do not. The boundaryless
benefits which participants reported emphasized new learning. In
conceptualizing the learning gained, participants focused on technical, professional, managerial, and interpersonal skills. The most
frequently cited category was the direct acquisition of new skills and
understanding (essentially knowing-how) through performing the
job. This was mentioned in connection with almost 60 percent of all
jobs. Other benefits were divided between getting to know oneself
better, or reported increases in breadth of view, or personal growth
(knowing-why), or getting to know others better (knowing-whom).

The characteristic accumulation of knowing-how learning was
aptly illustrated by Albert (Chapter 4), in his early experiences as a
young civil engineer, as he answered the repeated question, "What
did you get [from that job]?":

> *First job*: I was starting to get a bit of work history and work experience,
> learning what it's like being in the workforce. I was exposed to the
> construction industry which I knew I had an interest in. I didn't get a lot of
> job satisfaction from it, it ended up being quite boring and I knew it wasn't
> the firm I wanted to stay with, but I knew I needed the experience.

> *Second job*: I was offered a lot more variety, I was dealing with site
> supervision, coordinating everything from making sure the partitioning
> systems were on site to the men being there at the right time, so I was
> learning organizational abilities, supervision . . . [From the course work] I
> learned technical aspects, the formal aspects, how to approach it properly.
> We covered both the construction side and the quantity surveying side . . .
> it meant I could go on site and have the knowledge.

> *Third job*: I got a wider exposure to the actual construction side of things, I
> learned how to deal with the contractors and sub-contractors. I was getting
> more technical knowledge from the firm. It helped with my studies being
> broader.

In describing his own accumulation of competencies, Albert talks
mainly about competencies such as technical knowledge, industry
awareness, interpersonal and supervisory skills – in other words,

knowing-how. Little was mentioned at this stage of the interview that could be classed as knowing-why or knowing-whom.

Benefits in Knowing-Why

As shown in the above example, people emphasized their development of knowing-how competencies through the way they talked about the benefits they got from their jobs. Knowing-why and knowing-whom competencies were mentioned in a much lower proportion of cases. People were less conscious of their motivations unless something went wrong in their workplace, or they felt for other reasons it was time to move on. Similarly, people were more aware of the influences of knowing-whom at times of job transition. People also revealed their knowing-why and knowing-whom competencies through their reflections – their retrospective sensemaking (Chapter 3) – after enacting changes in employment arrangements.

Most changes of job, as we showed in Chapter 2, are voluntary. In describing these changes, the participants in our study typically answered the question "How did that change come about?" by describing not just *how* the change occurred but *why* it occurred and *who* was involved. Thus, knowing-why motivations (e.g. "I couldn't stomach that kind of autocracy any more") provided the motivation to change, and knowing-whom connections (e.g. "I called the boss of our client company to see if they had any vacancies") provided the network apparatus for change.

As we have previously noted, a number of reasons to change jobs, most often during the early career years, involved travel. People reported going away, moving around, and then returning to, or settling in, the geographic region under study. The root motivation to "see the world" often led to enduring career effects which became embedded in people's knowing-why identities. For example, Kirsty's (Chapter 4) experience abroad in a flower shop opened her eyes to the world of retailing in which she now owns her own store. Owen's (Chapter 4) experience with fish farming in Europe led him toward becoming an oyster farmer when he returned. Bruce's (Chapter 3) emergent people skills through running a bar led on to a successful career in sales. Another example is Maggie, whose involvement in the restaurant business prepared her to take a senior position in that business once she returned. Moreover, travel and relocation usually occurred on people's own volition, rather than on behalf of any employer company.[16]

Another group of moves involved motivations to accommodate family, either relocating with a spouse, or to be with a prospective spouse (Chapter 5). Where spouses and families were already established, there were several situations, like those of Barbara, Anne (Chapter 6), Elsie (Chapter 5), and Marie (Chapter 3) where people would move on to a new job that was more conveniently located and provided better hours to accommodate a family.

A third group of moves involved career adaptation or resilience. Although we have noted that layoffs among research participants were relatively rare, that does not mean that job situations remained unchanged. In a number of cases, people reported adjusting their knowing-why motivations, and taking the initiative to change employment arrangements to adapt to changing circumstances. For example, Desmond (Chapter 4) leaving his transportation manager's position to take up winemaking, Oliver (Chapter 6) giving up on a prospective partnership in the insurance business, and Annette (Chapter 5) resigning her teaching position because of excessive demands are all examples of this kind of career adaptation. Other reports of Sam (Chapter 6) and Norman (Chapter 6) resigning because of responsibilities taken away or denied to them represent a different kind of adaptation.[17]

A fourth category of moves was made in direct discomfort about the circumstances of the job, and the behavior of one's boss or colleagues, with a resultant desire to move into more agreeable employment circumstances. Examples include care worker Jennie (Chapter 6) saying she moved on because her boss was "a prick," retailer Kirsty (Chapter 4) recounting that her father's new partner "was being sly and trying to take our customers from behind our back," accountant Sam (Chapter 6) who "never got the feeling the company I worked for was very ethical," and plasterer Bruce (Chapter 3) quickly leaving a boss who "knew I was good [and] thought he could use me."

However, by far the largest group were those who reflected on both sides of the employment change, on what had become wrong with the previous job, and what seemed right about the next one. There was a consistency between both sides of the story, a pattern to the retrospective sensemaking that contributes to the enactment process. Catherine (Chapter 2) once more provides a useful example. She was highly aware of her knowing-why motivation to escape being "branded" (her own term) by unwanted stereotypes: first as an accountant (her original training); second as an academic (her longest-service job); and third as a specialist in telecommunications or a company servant of the telecommunications company. The early stabilization of Catherine's knowing-why motivation, concerned with becoming an all-round marketing professional, served as a base for a deliberate accumulation of experiences that was both focused and opportunistic.

Table 7.3 *Mechanisms used to find new jobs with new employers*

Type of mechanism	No. of instances
Formal	42
Personal networks	66
Combined formal and personal	13
Not ascertained	31
Total	152

Benefits in Knowing-Whom

The power of knowing-whom as an apparatus to change employers is demonstrated in some simple statistics from the 152 employer changes indicated over the research period (Table 7.3).

Of the 121 moves where we were able to ascertain whether the new job had been obtained formally or through networks 66 (55%) had been mediated mainly by personal network mechanisms, while a further 13 (11%) had involved personal networks together with formal mechanisms. These figures show the power of network contacts, spanning family, friends, social connections, and cumulative ties through work over their developing careers. They confirm the practical conclusion of a well-known job-hunter's guide that the most effective way to get a job interview is to use a personal contact to help to set it up.[18]

We were struck by the frequency with which these moves depended on chance encounters, often with contacts from some time back in the career actor's history. For example Ron, the cigarette salesman, had got his current job through a chance encounter with a man he had last seen when they had worked together 15 years before. However, mention of new career contacts was only rarely cited in reports of what people "got" from their jobs. For many, the accumulation of "knowing-whom" contacts may be more of a subconscious than a conscious career activity. Perhaps this reflects the era of the Industrial State in which we were led to believe that the corporation would provide, and that employment mobility and personal networks outside the corporation were unimportant. But most people relied on their personal networks, whether consciously developed or not, in finding new jobs.

Tying Career Competencies Together

A graphic example of knowing-whom competencies, and also of the close integration of the different career competencies, was Darren.

A Driving Ambition

Darren is 28. His career so far has been totally in the transportation industry. Darren's grandfather was a truck driver. His father is a truck driver, who has won prizes in truck-driving competitions. His uncles and his sister are also truck drivers. Darren knew from a young age that he wanted to follow the family tradition.

Darren has had five jobs, all in transportation companies. The first, when he was still too young to have a licence to drive trucks, was as a loader. His last four jobs have all been truck-driving jobs. The first two were arranged for Darren by his father, in companies he worked for. But eventually Darren decided that "it was time to hop out of my father's shoes." He wanted to start long-distance driving. Two owner-driver contacts, who had "seen what I did and what I could do" offered him a good job, but said they wouldn't be ready for him to start for a year. In the meantime, they directed him to a suitable job with another company, and he got it.

After a year, he left that company and joined the two owner-drivers, as previously arranged. He was well paid and well treated. He drove a high quality truck which won a major truck competition. He wanted to be recognized not just as a driver but as a top quality driver.

But after three years the owner-drivers were bought out by a larger company. Darren was kept on the staff. "But it was never the same after that . . . at the end of the day you were just a number." A friend at another long-distance company, Trucktrans, got him an interview, and he was offered a job immediately. Darren says all good drivers get their jobs by word of mouth.

Darren is proud of his expertise and clear about the benefits that it provides to his employer: "I don't think I've learned a heck of a lot out of Trucktrans. I think I've taught them a lot. You know, axle loadings for weight so you don't get a ticket, restraining loads which I basically learned when I was loading trailers. There was hardly anyone at Trucktrans who knew how to load a truck properly or restrain one properly. So I've taught a number of drivers to be more professional in their working environment."

Darren's involvement with truck-driving and truck drivers extends far beyond the sphere of work. As he puts it, "everything revolves round" the transportation industry in his house. Most of his friends are drivers. He and his wife go to parties with other drivers and their wives. They go to truck shows (where, like his father, Darren has started to win prizes). He has got truck-driving jobs with Trucktrans for a number of his friends. His pre-school daughters play with toy trucks.

In looking to the future, Darren concedes that he may eventually give up driving. But he will remain in the industry: "Move into the office, every now and then I help out in the office with dispatching. But I wouldn't want to be a dispatcher, I would rather be a fleet manager."

The most compelling feature of Darren's career is the strength of his knowing-whom networks, which involve his extended and nuclear family, each company that he has worked for, his social circle, and the industry generally. These networks overlap and interweave closely, and reinforce his knowing-why identity and knowing-how truck-driving skills. Darren can enact the thread of his career, and build career capital, through the interplay and mutual reinforcement of his principal career competencies. His further career progress will depend on his reputation and his industry links. As he expands his competencies from "truck-driving" to "the transportation industry" as a unifying theme in his career, he is likely to move closer to the future to which he aspires.

At the same time, we should be aware of the weaknesses in Darren's position. His eggs are invested very much in one basket. His family background has provided a firm base for a developing career, but it may at the same time have constrained him from seeing wider opportunities and appreciating his own potential. His knowing-why motivations are clear, but narrow. His knowing-how skills are extensive, but specialized. His knowing-whom networks are strong, but not wide. Yet the most valuable career networks may be those which involve a wide range of company, industry, and social contacts.[19]

Consider what might go wrong in Darren's career. He himself concedes that, although he has contributed to the learning of his present employer, he has learned little from the association. In respect of new learning, his career may be in the doldrums. He and his wife are both concerned about the long and anti-social working hours truck-driving involves. Darren may be accumulating further competencies off the job, but if he wants to ensure the continued accumulation of career capital, he perhaps needs to cultivate greater flexibility in his career and project investments.

However, if there are potential problems in Darren's career story, the story is at the same time a wonderful example of the enactment by Darren, and others, of not just a company but a whole industry. One can make a good case that the substance and strength of the industry is not derived, as management textbooks might have us believe, from rational strategy-making by managers seeking to fill market gaps. An alternative hypothesis is that the transportation industry is a massive, full-blown outcome of the enactment of careers by Darren and myriad others.

It is easy to see how Peter (Chapter 1) has enacted a software company, and Gus (Chapter 3) a stevedoring company, and Vera (Chapter 4) a nut business. They were founding entrepreneurs. The notion that, in their career behavior, ordinary workers like Darren can enact whole industries, is inherently more exciting. It is to that

kind of phenomenon, the collective fruits of individual career investment, that we proceed in Chapter 8.

Notes

1. Schein, E.H. *Career Dynamics: Matching Individual and Organizational
Needs*. Reading, MA: Addison-Wesley, 1978.

2. Hall, R. The strategic analysis of intangible resources. *Strategic
Management Journal*, 1992, 13: 135–44.

3. We use the term "understanding" here, rather than "knowledge", to
preserve the term knowledge for broader usage consistent with the three
"ways of knowing" involved in knowing-why, knowing-how, and knowing-
whom.

4. DeFillippi, R.J. and Arthur, M.B. The boundaryless career: a
competency-based perspective. *Journal of Organizational Behavior*, 1994,
15 (4): 307–24. (Revised in M.B. Arthur and D.M. Rousseau (eds.) *The
Boundaryless Career: A New Employment Principle for a New Organizational Era*.
New York: Oxford University Press, 1996.) See also Arthur, M.B., Claman,
P.H. and DeFillippi, R.J. Intelligent enterprise, intelligent careers. *Academy of
Management Executive*, 1995, 9 (4): 7–22.

5. Baker, B. MCI management competencies and the APL. *Journal of
European Industrial Training*, 1991, 15 (9): 17–27. Quinn, R.E. *Beyond Rational
Management*. San Francisco: Jossey-Bass, 1988.

6. Weick, K.E. and Berlinger, L.M. Career improvisation in self-designing
organizations. In M.B. Arthur, D.T. Hall and B.S Lawrence (eds.) *Handbook of
Career Theory*. New York: Cambridge University Press, 1989.

7. Leana, C.R. and Feldman, D.C. *Coping with Job Loss*. New York:
Lexington Books, 1992.

8. Marshall, J. *Women Managers: Moving On*. London: Routledge, 1995.

9. Handy, C. *The Age of Unreason*. Boston, MA: Harvard Business School
Press, 1989.

10. Weick, K.E. Enactment and the boundaryless career: organizing as we
work. In Arthur and Rousseau, op. cit. (4), pp. 40–59, 116–31.

11. Jones, C. Careers in project networks: the case of the film industry. In
Arthur and Rousseau, op. cit. (4), pp. 58–75; DeFillippi, R.J. and Arthur, M.B.
Paradox in project-based enterprise: the case of film-making. *California
Management Review*, 1998, 40 (2): 125–39.

12. Freeman, E.R. and Gilbert, D.R. *Corporate Strategy and the Search for
Ethics*. Englewood Cliffs, NJ: Prentice-Hall, 1988, p. 165.

13. Peters, T. *Liberation Management*. New York: Knopf, 1992, p. 223.

14. Weick, op. cit. (10).

15. Herzberg, F., Mausner, B. and Snyderman, B.B. *The Motivation to Work*.
New York: Wiley, 1959.

16. Inkson, K., Arthur, M.B., Pringle, J.K. and Barry, S. Expatriate assignment versus overseas experience: contrasting models of human resource
development. *Journal of World Business*, 1997, 14 (4): 151–68.

17. Waterman, R.H., Waterman, J.A. and Collard, B.A. Toward a career-

resilient workforce. *Harvard Business Review*, 1994, 72 (4): 87–95. We note that the high degree of resilience demonstrated among the research participants precedes the recent fashionability of the idea.

18. Bolles, R.N. *The 1996 What Color is Your Parachute*. Berkely, CA: Ten Speed Press, 1996. Using personal contacts has a long history. The proportion of cases using personal networks to change companies reported here is similar to that reported in Granovetter's classic work on "weak ties." Granovetter, M. *Getting a Job*. Boston: Harvard University Press, 1974.

19. Raider, H.J. and Burt, R.S. Boundaryless careers and social capital. In Arthur and Rousseau, op. cit. (10), pp. 187–200.

8 Investing Career Capital in Social Institutions

Sailing!

Martin was an avid yachtsman by the time he was ten, and won a national competition before finishing high school. He also showed an aptitude for the physical sciences, and after school took a job as a lab technician while studying engineering part-time. He began to sell sailboards for extra income, with some success. A few years later he left his employer to take up a sailing opportunity he couldn't combine with his work. After that, he was approached by a boatbuilding company to make masts for them. He did not like the company's offer but, encouraged by his experience with sailboards, he determined that there might be an opportunity for him to become a mastmaker in his own right. He started small, but his sailing reputation helped him to get orders. Three years later he took on another sailor/engineer friend with a stronger marketing orientation as his partner, and the business started to expand.

Martin has persisted with a dual sailing and boatbuilding career for the past 12 years. He has often taken time away from work to pursue sailing assignments. He is now married to another sailor, and his two young children are beginning to participate in their parents' recreational passion. Martin's contacts, and his reputation as both a well-known competitive sailor and a skilled boatbuilder have been helpful for his business, even though he does not sail the category of boats on which most of his business depends. He also knows his business success is dependent on his technical proficiency, and that "people wouldn't want to use my products if they didn't trust me" on technical matters. He takes particular pride in the number of repeat orders he has received from satisfied customers. Martin is increasingly involved as an agent for related products, and packages those products as subassemblies for larger boatbuilding activities. His business now earns a substantial part of its income from agency activities, selling to both industry competitors and end customers. He sees opportunities for further expansion in this area.

The sailing industry is Martin's life and passion. His home city has a leading reputation as a center for both competitive and leisure sailing activities. He describes the city as "the only place to be" to stay in that industry in his country. He adds that "the whole business is linked – we subcontract work to others, others subcontract work to us." Local customers understand these linkages and discriminate among them in placing new orders. Meanwhile, industry participants collaborate in their merchandising efforts overseas. It is common for overseas customers to sign a contract for a whole boat with one local firm. Thereafter, the work is divided up among local collaborators in an apparently seamless set of delivery arrangements.

Martin's career interfaces with a number of key social institutions. Most obviously, it interfaces with the *company* (his own company) in which his career is currently located. Second, he engages in a specialized *occupation*, and an associated set of occupational skills, as an engineer and mastmaker. Third, he develops networks and relationships with other participants in his *industry*, in this case boatbuilding. Fourth, he interacts with the encompassing social arena – *society* at large – through his family and recreational pursuits, which are still linked to his company, occupation, and industry.

These four arenas of career activity – company, occupation, industry and society – repeatedly provide the context for the careers of our research participants. They are arenas in which Martin is not only accumulating fresh career capital, but also, as this chapter will explore, *investing* the career capital he has already built.

Institutional Contexts for Career Behavior

Martin founded and contributed to his own small firm. He stands as the antithesis of the old "organizational career" model. However, Martin's story illustrates that his career does not lack for other institutional contexts. Company, industry, occupation, and society are all deeply interwoven with the texture of Martin's career. These same kinds of institutions are deeply woven into Rosabeth Kanter's ideas about new career logics, which we briefly introduced in Chapter 1. We will draw upon these career logics below, in exploring the four kinds of institutional contexts to which careers can relate.

The Company: Kanter argues that "bureaucratic careers" are characterized by a logic of company advancement. According to this kind of institutional logic, "all of the elements of career opportunity" – responsibility, challenge, influence, formal training and development, compensation – are closely tied to formal rank in a company employment system.[1] The company's institutional system makes direct assumptions about the link between employment rank and ability, and assigns pay and privileges accordingly. It simultaneously constrains career opportunities for a number of "stuck" employees, commonly blue-collar and clerical workers, who are viewed as having "limited or non-existent advancement potential."[2] Kanter observes that this kind of career persists, even if its hey-day is past. Moreover, as we noted in Chapter 1, the company remains a favorite focus of contemporary studies of career phenomena.

The Occupation: What Kanter calls professional careers are grounded in a logic of occupational specialization. The institutions of occupational or professional life – trade unions, professional associations, and more informal means of affiliation – provide the yardsticks for career progression. People advance through "the chance to take on ever-more demanding or challenging or important or rewarding assignments that involve greater exercise of the skills that define the professional's stock-in-trade."[3] In contrast, being "stuck" involves being denied the opportunity to demonstrate or enhance one's occupational ability, for example when workers on production lines or nurses in hospitals are constrained by minutely detailed job descriptions. It is predicted that investing career capital in occupational institutions will become more popular because of the potential to offer growth without further widening, heightening, or displacing people within any organizational pyramid.[4]

The Industry: Martin's career is strongly identified with, and dependent on, one industry – sailing. Kanter does not explore the idea of "industry careers," although she does stress the kind of inter-firm networking – pooling, allying, and linking across companies – through which industry arrangements unfold. A more direct emphasis on industry is to be found in the work of other writers, among them Michael Porter.[5] Porter's central argument is that close industry ties, commonly reinforced by regional proximity among firms and their customers, contribute to a dynamic set of industry arrangements from which, as in Martin's boatbuilding example, multiple parties benefit. Other writers have endorsed the central significance of industry, or industry region, as a principal institutional form behind the New Economy.[6] The argument may be made, as it has been for California's high technology Silicon Valley, that an industry, rather than any of its participating companies, may be the principal context for people's career behavior.[7]

Society: A further institutional context is society at large. Society hosts career behavior which may have indirect economic value but is not normally included in popular conceptions of the work arena. Some simple examples involve people's commitments to families, voluntary social services, local communities, and political associations. Kanter shows her concern for this arena in her comments on the "macro-social consequences" of career forms.[8] Martin engages with society through his sailing, which provides social benefits for himself, his family, the sailing crews with which he associates, and the wider sailing and general community in which he acts as a role model and promoter of the sport he loves. Society is often the beneficiary of the expression of personal values in people's career choices, and people's wider social and non-work roles.[9] The social context provides the host system within which company, occupational, and industrial career systems function, and lends broader meaning to careers grounded in those alternative contexts.

The Enactment of Institutions

The preceding discussion suggests a set of four principal institutional contexts – company, occupation, industry, society – in which careers function. Much of this book has highlighted how institutional contexts, and in particular employer company contexts, have influenced the enactment of people's careers. However, the idea of reciprocal influences flowing back to the job, and so to the employer company, is fundamental to enactment theory. In Chapter 7 we explored some of these reciprocal benefits in cataloguing the benefits to companies which research participants reported. We also noted earlier in this book how, as participants' careers progressed, they frequently carried their accumulated career competencies with them across company, occupational, industrial, and geographic boundaries. The suggestion from these earlier examples, as well as Martin's example, is that people don't just influence employer companies, but also influence the broader institutional arrangements through which both careers and companies function. If this is so, then how does this come about?

Stephen Barley offers a cyclical model of how the enactment of careers functions, shown in adapted form in Figure 8.1.[10] The first phase of the model portrays how *individual actions* unfold into the kind of career *stories* anticipated in Chapter 3 and reported throughout this book. These stories in turn influence the *institutional forms* in which people are making career investments. For example, the story of Martin's unfolding career in boatbuilding has given rise to a new institution – the company he founded. However, the engineering acumen of Martin and other mastmakers will also have influenced institutional arrangements in their chosen occupation. At a broader level the collaboration among mastmakers and other occupational specialists will have influenced institutional arrangements in the boatbuilding industry as a whole. In addition, Martin has been visible in society as a sailor and a parent, and will have had the opportunity to influence society's overall engagement with sailing as a form of recreation.

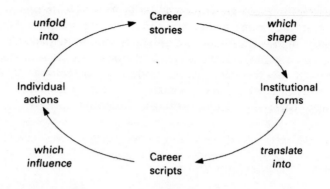

Figure 8.1   *The enactment of careers and institutional effects*

The second phase of the model describes how institutional forms give rise to career *scripts*, also briefly anticipated in Chapter 3. These scripts in turn influence the individual actions that people take in their careers. To stay with Martin as an example, he admits that he has been constrained by obligations to his own company in his work and complementary leisure pursuits. His career has also been affected by established occupational and industry arrangements in boatbuilding, from which he learned his part and took his cues in enacting his own career. In addition, Martin will have been influenced by sailing's prominent place in society, and the encouragement it provides to become a competitive hero, or a recreational participant, on society's terms.

Institutions and Career Competency Investments

In exploring the interplay between the enactment of careers and institutional arrangements we go beyond the focus of Chapter 7 on career capital accumulation. We are not only interested in the evidence of reciprocal effects on the company, but also in effects on other forms of institution as well. The preceding four chapters provided much evidence of people using one employment situation to anticipate another into which they could transfer their accumulated career capital. Moreover, the evidence in those chapters covered diverse examples of using jobs to gather not only company experiences but also occupational, industrial, and social experiences along the way. Like Martin, many of our research participants appeared to have a stake in these broader institutional arenas through which their careers unfolded.

Accordingly, our interest here is not in the accumulation of career capital itself, but in its further investment in the institutional realm. We extend the analogy between career capital and financial capital accumulation (Chapter 7) to the further question of capital investment. We may ask what use is financial capital until it has been invested? And what implications does that investment have for the companies or causes involved? Similarly, we may ask what patterns of career capital investment are visible from our research data? And, we may ask what do those patterns tell us about the enactment of the institutional realm – of companies, occupations, industries, and society at large – through which careers unfold?

Our interest here also extends Charles Handy's previously cited ideas about portfolio careers. Handy's point about portfolio careers is to look after oneself, to act with agency rather than communion in asserting and building one's own career capital. He further writes that "the portfolio life won't be to everyone's taste" as people search for new employment arrangements to replace the old company ones. We suggest that a broader view of institutional arrangements, spanning companies, occupations, industries, and not least society, allows wider possibilities for portfolio careers to be seen. These possibilities span the multiple institutions, including the institution of society, in which career capital investments can be made. The very point of a career may be to value and reinforce, rather than reject and dismantle, the institutional arrangements with which we most identify.

In extending this argument, it is important to note that the analogy between financial and career capital ought not to be taken too far. In particular, investors of financial capital are frequently passive, and without a direct presence at the investment site. In contrast, investors of career capital are both present and engaged with their adopted institutional venues. The grounds often used to criticize financial capital investments, citing such phenomena as "faceless owners" or "absentee landlords," explicitly do not apply to career capital investing. In career capital investing, people both join in and act through the institutions that they affect.

While it is important to keep in mind the full model of the interplay between individual actions and institutional forms, it is also important to note that the second part of the model has received by far the most attention. Both career theory and practice are replete with ideas of how companies (and their job descriptions), occupations (and their qualification and ranking systems), and industries (and their established business arrangements) contribute to the definition of career opportunities. However, the question of how the enactment of careers influences institutional forms has received less attention. In the rest of this chapter we will explore the evidence for this kind of influence. To do so, we will return to the career stories we collected from our 75 research participants.

Investing in the Company

Let us begin by looking at what it means to suggest that individual career investments build company institutions. As noted in Chapter 1, we use the term "company" to cover the economic unit in which a career actor is employed. Thus, the "company" may be a typical private sector employer, a person's place of self-employment, or a public sector or not-for-profit institution such as a high school (Janice), law court (Elaine), or church parish (Nigel). Take a case from Chapter 6.

Kelly had held a variety of positions, most recently as a marketing assistant, before she joined a temporary help agency in her late thirties and was placed with Fotex, a multinational office equipment company. She soon took a permanent secretarial position with Fotex on the understanding she would progress to a marketing assistant's position. Eighteen months later, Kelly was given the position she sought, but shortly after the company was restructured and moved most of its marketing work overseas. Kelly then volunteered to become a secretary again, to work for a technical services manager who was coming to her building. Nine months later Kelly was offered a position as a customer service representative. She still does that work, as well as coordinating her own and two other service representatives' work. Kelly is now 48 and has been with Fotex 12 years. Much of her energy, however, is focused on outside leisure interests. Following a dissolved marriage and other failed personal relationships, she hopes in due course to find a new long-term relationship. She has never seriously thought of leaving Fotex, or the customer relationships which now mean so much to her, and hopes to continue with the company until she retires.

This is Kelly's story from her perspective. We did not interview anyone at Fotex to determine how the company viewed Kelly's ongoing contribution and her current competence in customer training. Had we done so, however, the same story might have sounded like this.

Some years ago Fotex had a shortage of secretarial staff and made regular use of workers from a temporary help agency. Kelly came from the agency as a secretary, had good skills and a positive attitude, and was able to demonstrate the value of her past marketing experience. Fotex offered Kelly a permanent secretarial position, and later a marketing assistant's position which she held until most of the work was moved overseas. However, Kelly then volunteered to be a secretary again, and helped our technical services manager to secure his department in a difficult transitional period. The manager later needed a customer training representative to build client relationships and familiarity with the products. Kelly's interpersonal skills were high and she was given the job. Since then the function has expanded and been professionalized, due to company growth, technological change, and Kelly's own efforts. She now has a leadership role, and two subordinates whom she has personally socialized to understand the company's products and values. Much of Fotex expertise in a critical customer area is now vested in Kelly. She knows the company, its products and our local customers well, and we hope she continues to work for us.

Kelly's story describes the enactment of an individual career on behalf of the company, the host institution with which she now identifies. Kelly's primary (knowing-why) motivation is to serve her company. Her (knowing-how) skills perform the company's work. Her principal (knowing-whom) contacts are within the company, or on the company's behalf with customers. At a collective level, we can imagine the career stories of Kelly and other Fotex employees coming together to enact the company itself. However, Kelly's career is also about responding to company scripts. She accepts jobs that the company has available, rather than asserting her career preferences in more original ways.

The traditional Industrial State model sees the private company as the dominant host institution for careers, which unfold in an ascending hierarchy of responsibility and influence. Yet few people in our sample appeared to reflect such careers. Kelly's movement in Fotex was upward, but also lateral. Desmond made early progress in a transportation company but left when the stress became too great. Paula left a successful corporate career to work in her husband's business. Priscilla moved up in her design company, but more by virtue of informal expertise than formal rank. Peter's career in Infotex was terminated by the closure of the company.

A number of other people attempted to build their careers in private companies with limited success. Piers (Chapter 6) invested in an engineering company for years as a skilled machinist; failing eyesight forced him off his job but he was kept on and now works as a storeman. Similarly Gail (Chapter 6), a 20-year company administrator, tried when younger to gain inclusion in the company's decision-making circles; her attempts were frustrated, but she continues to serve the company in a modest role. In these cases, we can see people's earlier investments in enacting their careers giving way to larger acceptance of company encoded work roles (scripts).

In other cases, the enactment of the careers of machinist Barry (Chapter 4), carpet mender Chu, and refuse collector Troy (Chapter 4) seems in each instance to be responsive to company-encoded scripts already in place. These people may be reasonably included among what Kanter calls "stuck" employees, strongly constrained by the kind of work that they do.[11] Sam (Chapter 6) attempted from a managerial role to make a massive long-term commitment to changing a bakery company. However, his efforts were not valued by the company and eventually he left in frustration.

Several research participants exhibit persistent investments in *public sector* or *not-for-profit* institutions. Elaine the court official is a good example of someone enacting new public sector systems through career behavior. In Chapter 6 we reported that Elaine "ensures that she moves to a new department within the court every few years. She takes pride in humanizing and de-bureaucratizing, as far as she can, long-standing systems in the departments she works in."

To Elaine, each new job or transfer within her job is a new challenge to develop the part of the institution for which she is responsible into a new form. Thus:

Department 1: When I walked into the _____ section it was paper here and paper there. I thought, well, paper is all very well but what you are dealing with here is problems which are all very real to the people who come here. . . . For example they're in a relationship which has become violent, somebody has taken their children and they want them back . . . So I looked at the paper and thought, what can we get rid of here? How can we change this and try to put in a smoother system? Some things I implemented then are still in place.

Department 2: With a backlog [of trials] like that, I thought, well, if you are waiting that long, by the time you get your people into court, the main witnesses have forgotten most of the details. . . . So in conjunction with the judges and the registrar I said, we need to get rid of the backlog, how about we set up some more? So we actually increased the number of courts, but we had to do something to ensure that they were fully staffed all the time, so you are not saying, "Right, we've got a trial today, oh, sorry, not ready today, I want to go back and do it again." And so . . . if [the lawyer] was not able to take the briefs we would assign someone else. The judge was a great supporter of that style and it worked. Then within a year, we were able to offer a trial next week if that's what you wanted.

And so, the story of Elaine's career becomes not just the story of Elaine's career. It is a story in which Elaine's career capital investments interweave with those of others to enact enduring court modernization. Regrettably, as we noted earlier, Elaine's reforming zeal may have been moderated by recent pressures for short-term productivity that have taken on-the-job learning opportunities away.

However, in most of the instances of career capital investments in a particular company there appears to be a parallel commitment to occupation. Long-term Fotex worker Kelly also has an occupational identity (as a trainer) and an industry identity (in the office equipment industry). She says that if she lost her job, she would look for a similar one, applying the same (knowing-how) skills in the same occupation, with a different company. Accounts clerk Gail sees her accounting (bookkeeping) skills as her stock-in-trade and harbors ideas about going into private practice, doing the books for small business clients. Court registrar Elaine stays with the only public sector institution in which she can practice her occupation. Similarly, not-for-profit sector workers in schoolteaching (Marie, Chapter 3; Janice, Chapter 6), higher education (Oliver, Chapter 6), human services (Gareth), the church (Nigel, Chapter 5), firefighting (Sargent, Chapter 4), and air traffic control (Quentin, Chapter 6), all persist in the limited employment situations catering to their adopted occupation. We focus next on these and other investments in occupational institutions.

Investing in an Occupation

Beyond the cases already mentioned in the preceding section, a cluster of some 18 participants have accumulated career capital invested principally in their occupations. They had either used their occupations as a source of career stability in a world of changing company arrangements, or used inter-company mobility to achieve occupational growth. These include: Barbara (physical therapist, Chapter 7), Catherine (marketer, Chapter 2), Darren (truck driver, Chapter 7), David (cabinet maker), Glenda (optometrist, Chapter 5), George (baker), Helen (occupational health specialist, Chapter 5), Henry (computer programmer, Chapter 5), Ron (salesperson, Chapter 6), Susan (marketer, Chapter 5) and Tommy (farm worker, Chapter 4). Several women (Anne, Chapter 6; Elsie, Paula and Vandanna, all Chapter 5) developed transferable secretarial and office skills, and two more (Annette, Chapter 5; Elisabeth, Chapter 6) pursued what might reasonably be called their principal occupation – homemaking.

These workers invested occupational career capital in a variety of situations. In each, the worker brought new occupational skills to bear, enacting change upon occupational practice. However, in each case the worker also developed further career competencies, building his or her stock of occupational career capital in the process. Barbara (Chapter 7) added new therapy skills in each of her mainstream hospital, maternity hospital, and rest home positions. Susan (Chapter 1) found the occupational identity she wanted as a marketer and now sees herself as a mobile professional, able to enact new approaches wherever she is needed. As suggested in our discussion of knowing-why motivations in Chapter 7, the mark of a confident occupational career is often inter-company, and even inter-industry, mobility.

While in these stories occupational institutions appear dominant, employer companies are still parallel beneficiaries of continuing career investments. In several cases, a strong sense of occupational career investment has paralleled a prolonged stay in a particular company. These include property manager Claudia, designer Priscilla (Chapter 3), computer consultant Stephen (Chapter 6), and welder Tony (Chapter 5). These employees enact company and occupational careers simultaneously.

Priscilla is a good example. She has stuck with her company through thick and thin, and has taken on just about every job inside the company. By doing so she has enacted her career indelibly on to the company and its other workers. But she has developed the occupational skills of a designer, and done so to the maximum extent possible within her one-company employment. Is hers a company or an occupational career? Priscilla also engages within her company's industry through her efforts to secure new business. Is hers an industry career too? If so she is not alone in investing simultaneously in three institutional contexts.

We close this section by noting that if people are to rely on occupational career investments, continuing occupational development is needed. Norman the accountant (Chapter 6) failed to upgrade his skills and now enacts involuntarily in the social sphere only. Henry the computer programmer (Chapter 5) failed to think strategically about the skills he was developing; he took the jobs that were convenient, and is now anchored in the airline industry, and worried that his skills may be out-of-date or not transferable beyond his industry.

Investing in Industry (and Occupation)

In many cases it was difficult to dissociate career actors' investments in industry from related investments in occupation. One group of cases involving regular employment (rather than self-employment) arrangements included Damien (catering industry, chef), Desmond (wine, winemaker) Jean (food, merchandizer), Maggie (hospitality, caterer), Sally (advertising, media planner), and Tina (clothing, retailer). Albert applies the combination twice over in his two current jobs (engineering industry, salesperson; hospitality industry, barman). Student Christine makes twin investments in human services and as a future special needs teacher. And of course there is also Darren (transportation, truck driver).

These people have spent much of their lives in their industries, and have varying degrees of love or hate for it. Truck driver Darren's (Chapter 7) life is intensely bound up with the transportation industry. Restaurant supervisor Maggie and chef Damien (Chapter 3) have made high investments in the restaurant industry. Assistant wine-maker Desmond (Chapter 4) has drifted back into the wine industry because of family connections. Merchandiser Jean (Chapter 5) has always had jobs loosely connected with food, but has little con-sciousness of the industry as a cohesive entity. Sally has made a major career investment in advertising, the only industry she has worked in, but having decided while she was expecting her first child that the industry simply didn't match up with her knowing-why values, she intended to start in something different.

From the stories of some of these actors – those in the catering and hospitality industries for example – one gets a strong sense of "industry community" as the real unit of analysis. These are not industries like electricity generation or paper-milling, dominated by a few strong players, but industries of myriad small firms. They are industries that can engage people's identities regardless of any par-ticular employment arrangements, and provide networks and learn-ing agendas emphasizing industry rather than either company or occupational concerns.

Another large group involved in parallel industry and occupa-tional investments are the self-employed workers. They include Alex (agriculture, farmer), Bill (entertainment, stagehand), Brett (construc-tion, plasterer), Cedric (computer services, stationer and consultant), Cliff (construction, builder), Gina (day care, manager), Gus (shipping, stevedore), Honor (agriculture, farmer), James (construction, tiler), Jennie (welfare, caregiver), Jeff (landscaping, landscaper), Owen (fisheries, oyster farmer), Peter (computing, software provider), Phillip (regional development, town planner) and Vera (farming, horticulturalist).

Self-employment represents an interesting hybrid case. Going into self-employment is often an attempt to leverage occupational career capital as a newly independent industry player. In the early years especially, people's occupational investments are often prominent, and provide for "employability" should the new company fail. For example, day-care proprietor Gina (Chapter 6) fits this category, since it was her direct skills in caring for children that moved parents to support her in starting a new center. Gina could surely get a job supervising someone else's facility if her self-employment initiative failed. Success in self-employment may then bring on a greater commitment to the industry, as in nut grower Vera's (Chapter 4) shift from being a farmer to being a food industry wholesaler. In contrast, for Jonathan, changing economic circumstances disrupted his success as a retailer, and he fell back, awkwardly, on his pharmacist skills.

Investing in the Social Arena

Traditional career theorists would argue that people seek out the work for which they are suited, and that as they exercise individual values and aptitudes through their unfolding careers, they create downstream benefits for the community. Numerous research participants, especially the men, viewed their careers in this way. For example, Peter (Chapter 1) noted that the software computer company in which he so powerfully enacted his own career also contributed considerably to the regional economy. A related theme, again common among the men in our sample, concerned financial provision for their families.

However, a separate kind of social investment came from others who made a more direct association between their work – including unpaid work – and its social effects. These actors made sense of their careers through directly shaping their investments toward some larger social or community good. In some cases – secretary Anne (Chapter 6), landlord Dan (Chapter 6), office managers Elsie and Paula (both Chapter 5), town planner Phillip (Chapter 4), and clerk Vandanna (Chapter 5) – a principal concern was the accommodation of their careers with parallel family investments. Many women, and some men, framed choice of employment location and working hours around the child-care needs of their families and the complementary availability of their partners. In so doing, they enacted the social arena on to the work arena.

Numerous participants, particularly women, brought to their career behavior a strong ethic of altruism, often within the fabric of voluntary community work. Part of therapist Barbara's *knowing-why* (Chapter 7) was strong empathy with her patients, a wish to support them and to learn from them. It seemed that as her career unfolded she grasped the opportunities to create a climate of support around her patients. This theme can be traced throughout her career as her client groups moved from hospital patients, to pregnant women to elderly people. Another conscious intent to serve was found in Janice's work (Chapter 6) as a guidance counsellor. Similarly, Christine's choice (Chapter 5) to train as a special needs teacher demonstrates a motivation of service in the social arena, which will no doubt be played out in her teaching practice. Other strong social and community investments could be identified in Elaine's (Chapter 6) court work, Jack's counselling (Chapter 4), Julie's union organizing (Chapter 4) and Nita's teaching (Chapter 4).

Two participants had enacted particularly strong personal values in the social arena through their careers.

Serving Life

Jennie raised five children, and then made the transition into paid work through volunteer work as a community worker assisting people with intellectual disabilities. She did job-sharing with her daughter and then took over the job full-time when her daughter had a baby. She admits that her early attitude to those with intellectual disabilities was that she "was doing them some big favor." However, her attitude changed to one of viewing her charges as equals, and from her work she got "trust, love and a great deal of satisfaction seeing other people's quality of life change and improve." She "pulled herself up by her bootstraps" as she developed her skills from volunteer to paid worker to manager to being self-employed. By the time of the interview she ran two houses for the intellectually disabled. She lived in one and worked over 100 hours a week. She commented "you give your soul really, it is a very demanding job." Jennie has become somewhat disillusioned and is seriously contemplating a change. As she says, "I love working with the people with an intellectual disability, but it just kills you, you can't do it forever, there is not enough money, there is not enough support."

Gareth was visually impaired, left school without qualifications, and as the condition slowly worsened moved to potential opportunities in a bigger city. As primary breadwinner of his young family he did repetitive work for ten years, but it wasn't satisfying or challenging. Through a former colleague, he was offered a social work job with his ethnic group. Gareth had no relevant qualifications but had excellent interpersonal skills. After a "quick baptism" and a few in-house courses, he began working as a field officer. His ethnic upbringing emphasized the value of collectivity so he established a network of client groups and their families that formed the first collective voice for this group. "I had some knowledge [but] I had people within my networks to call on for help." He used his social work role to sponsor community action rather than simply delivering services from an institutional base. He has since won a fellowship that has taken him overseas to learn from other indigenous peoples and to share a rehabilitation model that he helped develop, not as an expert, "but as a messenger for my peers." Gareth's own disability became the impetus for him taking on challenges, but it was the values of his ethnic group and their collective ways of working which enabled him to mobilize his community and to extend services throughout the country. His career capital rests directly on

his social capital networks around the country, and his fight for social
justice depends on the connections with others. He comments that he has
learned "power in people and that is the best way to move things forward,
collectively."

These two stories of career enactment, demonstrate almost incidental
beginnings: for Jennie, a desire to help and to share in an interest of
her daughter; for Gareth, a personal disability. From these somewhat
serendipitous starts grew a passion which fuelled these career actors
as they sought to help others to develop their potential more fully.
The present outcomes of the two stories show a different return on
the career investments in the social arena. For Jennie the persistent
financial inequity and lack of appreciation from the dominant institutions have led to emotional burnout and desire to make a change.
Gareth has been sustained by strong community networks, a growing
social and political awareness, and latterly, growing international
recognition for his work.

Jennie and Gareth exemplify the participants in our sample who
have made strong investments in the social arena. This career direction is coupled with social change for the disadvantaged groups with
whom our career actors are involved. All desire a suitable return on
their career investments and if the changes sought are not forth-
coming in the long term, then they realign their goals to demonstrate a
different institutional emphasis. Their passion is played out in the
social arena through varying levels of parallel investments in occupation, industry and company.

Combinations of Career Investments

The preceding discussion points to careers engaging with shifting
company, occupational, industrial, social, and institutional arrangements. As we noted in Chapter 2, the great majority of career moves
are voluntary, inter-company moves. Many involve a shift in occupation, industry, or geographic location. The broadest picture involves
the career at any one time being at the nexus of separate but overlapping company, occupational, industrial, and societal contexts
(Figure 8.2). However, any location on the figure provides only a
snapshot – a "still" of the "moving picture" of a career unfolding over
time. The snapshot will change each time a person changes company,
occupation, industry, location, or social arrangements.

As people move on, institutions worry: companies worry about
"labor turnover;" industries worry about "brain drain;" occupations

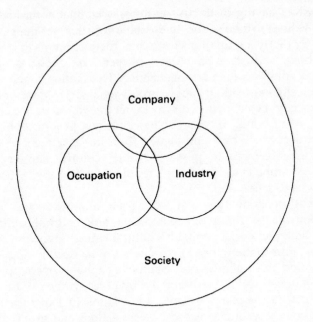

Figure 8.2   *Overlapping contexts in the enactment of careers*

worry about shortages of qualified people; and society worries about unstable home backgrounds. But as each type of institution worries, each also becomes a potential beneficiary of the job changes and the associated circulation of competencies that this chapter illustrates. As we have shown in Chapter 2, such changes are commonplace; as we have shown in Chapter 7, such changes also provide an opportunity for new knowledge transfer to the new institution.

The Institutionalization of Career Capital

To explore the effects of these investments further we return to the framework of career competencies introduced in Chapter 7. A company's core competencies involve capabilities that are critical for delivering its present production or service capabilities, as well as for promoting new learning endeavors. To recap, these core competencies may be categorized as combinations of company culture (its shared beliefs and values), know-how (its overall skills and comprehension) and networks (its supplier, customer, and alliance partner linkages).

A similar argument may be applied to the three other institutional contexts. Occupations, industries, and whole societies are commonly described as having distinctive cultures, identifiable through recognizable values, symbols, and understandings that set their members apart.[12] Similarly, occupations have their distinct claims to specialized "know-how," industries have their "recipes," and societies have their ingrained administrative arrangements.[13] Occupations and industries also typically network through professional or trade associations, while society hosts many network devices through its religious, political, recreational and charitable institutions. In sum, all four kinds of institution which host and benefit from the enactment of people's careers may be seen to possess distinct culture, know-how, and network "competencies" which are the lifeblood by which those institutions function.

Our culture, know-how and networks framework relates closely to Pierre Bourdieu's "forms of capital," spanning cultural capital, symbolic capital, and social capital.[14] Cultural capital involves "empathy towards, appreciation for, or competence in deciphering cultural relations and cultural artifacts." Symbolic capital – overlapping with what economists call human capital – involves symbols of intellectual ability such as degrees, awards, and claims to experience. Social capital involves resources based on connections and group membership.[15] These three forms of capital relate closely to the knowing-why, knowing-how and knowing-whom components of "career capital" that we have described at the individual level.

Another related approach comes from Anthony Giddens, and in particular from his notion of "knowledgeability" – essentially people's capacity to accumulate and act on knowledge as they go about their daily lives. This capacity for knowledge accumulation is "grounded in the continuous monitoring of action which human beings display and expect others to display."[16] Like our concept of career capital, it incorporates elements of self-knowledge (what we call knowing-why), practical knowledge (knowing-how), and knowledge of other human beings (knowing-whom). Also, like our concept of career capital, the capacity about which Giddens writes is seen as integral to the patterning of social life, and so of social institutions, with which it interacts.

Both Bourdieu's and Giddens' perspectives emphasize how people's subjective career behaviors influence macro-institutional forms, and lend support to the enactment of careers perspective that is central to this book. A third supporting perspective is that of the Chicago School of Sociology (introduced in Chapter 1).[17] The Chicago School also saw careers as a mediating force between the institutional realm and the day-to-day interactions of social life. However, the institutions were frequently not employing companies, for the Chicago School saw careers through a wider lens than that provided by the company perspective.

Table 8.1 *Institutional benefits stemming from the enactment of "knowing-why, knowing-how and knowing-whom" career capital investments*

	Company	Occupation	Industry	Society
Cultural capital	Investments in shared intra-company beliefs and values or in company-centered approaches to influence these through internal initiatives.	Investments in beliefs and values broadly shared among occupational members, or in pursuing a new vision of the occupation's role or mission.	Investments in beliefs and values broadly shared within an industry, or in promoting the industry's further interests in the larger economic world.	Investments in beliefs and values concerned with the welfare of society at large, and putting society's interests ahead of more limited economic interests.
Human capital	Investments in company-specific or company-prescribed skills and understanding, or assisting in developing new skills and expertise sets on the company's behalf.	Investments in occupation-specific skills and understanding, or in the promotion of new skills and expertise on the occupation's behalf.	Investments in industry-specific skills and understanding, or in the promotion of new approaches in the industry's greater interests.	Investments in skills and understanding deemed to have particular social value, and to promote broad social rather than constrained parochial outcomes.
Social capital	Investments in relationships with other company members or with outside partners, suppliers, or customers on the company's behalf.	Investments in relationships with other occupational members, and directed toward or justified to be in the occupation's overall interests.	Investments in relationships with or on behalf of members of the industry, and directed toward the collective interests of those members.	Investments in diverse relationships concerned for the maintenance or betterment of the social fabric and citizenship within that fabric.

Table 8.1 summarizes our arguments about how the enactment of people's careers, as reflected in their emergent knowing-why, knowing-how, and knowing-whom career capital investments, stands to benefit each of the four institutions we have discussed. For consistency of terminology, as well as for greater consistency with other social science perspectives, we label the three arenas of institutional benefit as cultural capital (instead of culture), human capital (instead of know-how) and social capital (instead of networks).[18]

An Integrative Example

To illustrate the interplay of career behavior and institutional effects, we offer the case of researcher Adrian.

Instituting career capital

Adrian has had a varied early career, including periods as a social worker, treasury officer, court reporter, and television journalist, followed by twelve years as a computer specialist in the government sector and eight years in his present company. He works in a department offering technology-based educational services to the health care industry. He describes his role as a "research sociologist" and gives his job title as "Director of Educational Resources", although in practice his title matters little.

Because of a phobia, Adrian is reluctant to seek employment elsewhere. But he has a strong need for novelty, and responds to it by constantly redefining his role. Initially he had editorial responsibilities that took advantage of both his computing and writing skills. But he soon found that his situation was not highly structured: "The job seemed to be flexible and open-ended. If I came up with any good idea I seemed to have the freedom to go ahead." He has since made resource kits, explored audio, video and Internet options for distance learning, become "the computer expert for the department" and "done graphic design for everything from banners to visiting cards." Adrian has exercised his influence throughout the educational and health care industries and also across the several occupations – teacher, computer systems developer, marketer, journalist – for which his work serves as a nexus. For information and social connections he networks with academics, technicians, photographers, graphic artists, and media people. He is involved in major projects, yet has flexibility in his hours, which is important to his family life. He loves this flexibility of hours, and comments that although his job is full-time "it sometimes feels like part-time." In the social arena he successfully meshes with the intermittent work hours of his wife and the needs of his daughter who has a medical condition.

Adrian's career story is underpinned by what he calls his "perpetual learner" philosophy. In addition to his paid work he is engaged in another postgraduate degree. Within his position he goes out of his way to find new projects from which he can learn. He sees his job as "moving forward from project to project . . . until I exhaust it in terms of its potential to do new and interesting things." This philosophy effectively takes Adrian across any real or imagined boundaries both within his company and beyond.

Adrian's story is one in which his continuing career capital investments are easily discerned. His knowing-why investments incorporate his perpetual learner philosophy, and accommodation of his phobia and his family life. His knowing-how investments, also driven by his perpetual learner philosophy, occur at the intersection of the distinctive occupational and industrial arenas in which he participates. His knowing-whom investments incorporate a diverse range of experts with whom he interacts as new work projects are accomplished.

However, the enactment of Adrian's career also adds to the competencies of each of the four kinds of institutions covered in this chapter. He contributes to his company's cultural capital (through his commitment to his work and his negotiation of family needs), human capital (through the added value of the new health care services he provides), and social capital (through his seeking of outside technical advice). Similarly, he contributes to the occupations (notably, computing and desktop publishing) and industries (education and health care) in which he participates and which are also richer for Adrian's presence. Finally, he contributes to society through the family investments he is able to make in parallel with his work.

To return to the model illustrated in Figure 8.1, the story of Adrian's career so far is one in which he has shaped each of the four kinds of institutional forms we have described. Moreover, the scripts stemming from those institutional forms in turn clearly have reflected Adrian's influence in the way he has done his job. In other words, Adrian's past career performance has helped to define the job duties he is presently asked to perform. These emergent duties – that is, career scripts – give rise to a new round of enactment in Adrian's unfolding career story.

Adrian's story is paralleled by other participants in this research. It is a story of people accumulating career capital through knowing-why, knowing-how, and knowing-whom competencies. It is a story of how that career capital becomes invested in institutions as cultural, human and social capital. It is as if the career actor can play the same three-suited hand of cards simultaneously at three or four different tables – the tables of his or her company, occupation, industry and society. However, in this card game both the player and the institutional dealer can win, and both are more likely to win provided new cards continue to be introduced. Those new cards come from the enactment of careers.

Notes

1. Kanter, R.M. (1989) Careers and the wealth of nations: a macro-perspective on the structure and implications of career forms. In M.B. Arthur, D.T. Hall and B.S. Lawrence (eds.) *Handbook of Career Theory*. New York: Cambridge University Press, 1989, p. 509.

2. ibid., p. 509.

3. ibid., pp. 510–11.

4. Tolbert, P.S. Occupations, organizations and boundaryless careers. In

M.B. Arthur and D.M. Rousseau (eds.) *The Boundaryless Career*. New York: Oxford University Press, 1996, pp. 331–49.

5. Porter, M.E. *The Competitive Advantage of Nations*. New York: Free Press, 1990.

6. Piore, M.J. and Sabel, C.F. *The Second Industrial Divide*. New York: Basic Books, 1984.

7. Saxenian, A. Beyond boundaries: open labor markets and learning in the Silicon Valley. In Arthur and Rousseau op. cit. (4), pp. 23–39.

8. Kanter, op. cit. (1), p. 520.

9. Kofodimos, J.R. *Balancing Act: How Managers Can Integrate Successful Careers and Fulfilling Personal Lives*. San Francisco: Jossey-Bass, 1993.

10. Barley, S.R. Careers, identities and institutions: the legacy of the Chicago School of Sociology. In Arthur, Hall and Lawrence, op. cit. (1), pp. 41–65.

11. Kanter, op. cit. (1), p. 509.

12. For example, Hansen, C.D. Occupational cultures: whose frame are we using? *Journal for Quality and Participation*, 1995, 18 (3), pp. 60–75; Phillips, M.E. Industry mindsets: exploring the cultures of two macro-organizational settings. *Organization Science*, 1994, 5 (3): 384–402.

13. Raelin, J. *Clash of Cultures*. Boston: Harvard University Press, 1991; Spender, J.C. *Industry Recipes*. Oxford: Blackwell, 1989.

14. Bourdieu, P. The forms of capital. In J. Richardson (ed.) *Handbook of Theory and Research for the Sociology of Education*. New York: Greenwood, 1986, pp. 241–58.

15. Bourdieu's fourth kind of capital, economic capital, lies outside the scope of this study.

16. Giddens, A. *The Constitution of Society*. Berkeley, CA: University of California Press, 1984, p. 3.

17. Barley, op. cit. (10).

18. For example, Sowell, T. *Race and Culture: A World View*. New York: Basic Books, 1994 (on cultural capital); Becker, G. *Human Capital*. New York: Columbia University Press, 1964 (on human capital); and Burt, R.S. *Structural Holes: The Social Structure of Competition*. Cambridge: Harvard University Press, 1992 (on social capital).

9 The Enactment of Careers: From Present to Future

Our objective in this book is to look at careers through a different lens. We are aware that the world in which careers are played out is changing rapidly. We are also aware that traditional lenses were never designed to highlight this change.

The traditional lenses suggested that people would stay with what they had been trained for, what they knew, what society seemed to designate for them. Vocational theories emphasized that people remain adjusted to their jobs and occupations. Adult development theories and career-stage theories suggested common frames to explain myriad career experiences. The management literature treated the career as a micro-tool of the Industrial State, a company-engineered device to protect productivity, reduce turnover, and perpetuate company hierarchies.

These aims, in their time, were worthy enough. However, the whole system depended on predictability and stability, qualities distinctly lacking in the emerging employment world. Nowadays some companies and workers seem to be reconstituting fragments of the deregulated, restructured, destructured Industrial State into new flexible forms of company or career. Or they seem to be clinging desperately to old assumptions, like survivors of a shipwreck, or simply getting cast aside as unwanted debris.

The old theories don't reflect the burgeoning mobility of economic life at the close of the twentieth century, nor the weakening of formal controls as employer companies strive to stay competitive. They don't have much to say about the casualties of economic changes – those who trusted the great institutions of the Industrial State and who were let down. They don't support our understanding of "boundaryless careers"[1] in which inter-company career mobility, often voluntary mobility, is more the rule than the exception. Most of all, they don't highlight how people can *enact* their own careers, in their own frameworks, and in the process contribute to, rather than simply respond to, the unfolding New Economy.

We wanted to hear the authentic voice of career actors as they described not just the objective career movements that they made, but the subjective quandaries, dramas, disappointments, and exhilarations of unfolding career activity. We wanted to know what careers felt like, how they unfolded, how they connected with the past, and how they anticipated the future. We wanted to know what careers meant in the wider context of people's lives, and how they related to the institutions of society. We wanted to hear people's own stories about their "emerging sequences of work experiences over time."[2] What we heard is now the substance of this book.

This final chapter has two parts. The first reflects on the principal themes and highlights in the substance of the findings we have so far reported; the second offers suggestions for the pursuit and accommodation of future careers in the New Economy.

People Are Mobile in Their Careers

In the early pages of this book, we traced the career paths of our participants by counting their jobs, their employers, and their job-to-job and employer-to-employer moves over a ten-year period. We noted whether these moves were voluntary or involuntary, intra-company or inter-company, and whether they resulted directly in career "advancement" as conventionally defined. We counted moves between industries, occupations, and geographical locations. We concluded that the workforce as represented by these individuals was mobile: eighty percent of our sample changed their employer at least once in a ten-year period. The average participant experienced about three different employers over the ten-year period.

Moreover, most moves were voluntary – people attempting to guide their own careers rather than responding involuntarily to powerful economic or corporate forces. People were also reasonably mobile between occupations – only 41 percent were in the same general occupation at the end of the ten years as they had been in at the beginning. About one third of inter-company moves involved a change of occupation, one third a change of industry, and one third a change of geographical location. We concluded that career theorizing based on conceptualizations of restrictive company or occupational chimneys was of dubious relevance in a world where non-linear careers appeared to be the rule rather than the exception.

How representative are the country and sample population of career actors explored in this book? Our research design was grounded in what were seen to be international, rather than local, career trends. The country we studied was seen by outside observers as being in the vanguard of adaptation to international economic factors such as trade and currency liberalization, reduction of government intervention in business, and de-nationalization of industry.[3] Its rate of employment mobility was similar to rates recently observed in Britain, the USA and Japan.[4] Our sample was more representative of the occupational spectrum, and of diversity within it, than most of the samples on which other career studies have been conducted. Putting the evidence together, we believe our findings on the enactment of careers are broadly applicable across countries participating in the New Economy. However, we caution that the interpretation of our findings will need to be moderated according to particular country circumstances (as has been illustrated by a similar recent study in France[5]).

People *Enact* Their Careers

Our principal theoretical framework has been Karl Weick's concept of *the enactment of careers*.[6] Enactment involves people's choices, and their actions in pursuit of those choices. As individuals enact their careers, they also enact the environment in which careers take place. As workplace boundaries and rules weaken, individual enactment takes on enhanced importance. People enacting their careers create their own career narratives or "stories" as a means of personal sense-making[7] in a shifting environment. Rather than "career planning" – except in the broadest sense – in the long term, people "career improvise" in the short term. They adapt and engage in ongoing career-relevant learning. Sometimes they enact by seeking to impose individual agency on a malleable environment; at other times, they enact in a communal frame, seeking to integrate with other people in a search for shared meaning.[8]

The enactment perspective enables a focus on career phenomena as processes rather than structures. The term "career" as a noun, despite our neutral definition, "the unfolding sequence of a person's work experiences over time,"[9] sometimes carries unwanted connotations of stability, permanence, dependence on paid work, and professional status. Curiously, the verb "to career," means "to swerve about wildly in an uncontrolled manner;" perhaps this goes too far in the opposite direction. But "to enact" is a transitive verb, which focuses on constructive individual behavior. We do not just "enact," we "enact *something*." We have eschewed the noun "organization" in the sense of a definable entity, "an organization," because of our view that "organization" is a process rather than a definable structure. Analogously, we find advantages in conceptualizing "careering" or at least "the enactment of careers" as a process which creates, but also constantly modifies, the structures of institutions and of individual lives.

The early career stories that we highlighted were selected to illustrate enactment. Peter, the persistent learner who participated in the downsizing of his former company, Catherine, the accountant turned academic turned marketer, and Gus, the laid-off stevedore who won the outsourced contract for his former job, all displayed a common characteristic. That characteristic was to make a difference in the world in which their careers unfolded, rather than to passively accept external events or prescriptions. Later career stories confirmed that this characteristic – the capacity for enactment – was present across the range of careers we explored.

Career Concerns Vary and Change

In the middle chapters of this book we reviewed, from research participants' own perspectives, the subjective narratives and meanings which people applied in enacting their careers. Their stories covered occupational and job choices and transitions, the integration of work careers with home and family, and reciprocal relationships between career actors and employers. We grouped reports according to a principle of "cycles within cycles," emphasizing macro career stages while acknowledging that they included more micro and more recurrent project cycles. We reported evidence of "fresh energy," such as in the case of Wendy, where exploratory and novelty-seeking behavior led her first into pharmaceuticals and then into marketing. We reported on "informed direction," where people like occupational nurse Helen found momentum and direction through purposeful accumulation of distinctive work experiences. We chronicled examples of "seasoned engagement," where people like technical specialist Oliver persistently sought to make the most of their previous career experiences, and to ride out the turbulence of a changing world.

The variation in career concerns was perhaps most evident in our findings about "fresh energy." People seldom found their way into one "right" career opportunity. Instead, they experimented, sometimes in an apparently directionless way, as they learned about themselves and the world of work. Discontinuity was often a virtue. Opportunities were likely to present themselves through individual curiosity or by chance, rather than because of planning. People travelled to satisfy personal rather than company agendas, with the full value of travel as preparation for new career directions not becoming apparent until later. Some rejected status and salary advancement and instead sought lower-paid learning opportunities in "self-designed apprenticeships." For others, more constrained to "put bread on the table," a desire for novelty and learning often still underlay their career behavior.

The pursuit of "informed direction" was also symptomatic of the new, more flexible career forms. There were relatively few in our sample who appeared to depend largely on career-long investments in a single company or occupation. It was more usual to make intermediate investments in occupational or company advancement, and to interweave work career tracks with the responsibilities, supports, and complementary experiences provided by home, partner, and family. Others made it clear that their primary commitment was to the unpaid work of caring for their families, or that their career direction stemmed from their own ideals or interests, or from subsidiary activities such as volunteer work or hobbies. Finding or re-finding informed direction was seldom an unwavering planned activity. Rather, it emerged powerfully from sensemaking about the past and from the comfort or discomfort of the present.

In "seasoned engagement," people sought to take advantage of the career choices and experiences they had previously made. Some, like accountant Norman, appeared ill-prepared for the external changes taking place. Others stuck with employers who continued to practice the old virtue of mutual loyalty, but these employees tended to be adaptable in their contributions. However, the more successful career stories appeared to combine the leveraging of experience with the versatility to apply that experience in new ways, for example in Cedric's new business and Elaine's court system reforms. Through this versatility, the macro-cycle of the career gave rise to new micro-cycles of project activity. For older workers, though, the new activities often placed a higher premium on lifestyle and family concerns. A common theme among these participants was that of "holding on" through incremental adaptation to change.

Careers Are Simultaneously Continuous and Discontinuous

Careers are apparently continuous. They reflect developing identities, and draw upon deeply rooted characteristics of ethnicity, class, gender, and family background, as well as on unfolding and irreversible work experience. Careers interact with home life and other unpaid pursuits; these commonly remain in place while jobs and careers change. Even the causes of career changes, such as the desire to continue to learn, or to stay closer to one's family, or to seek out new horizons, often reflect continuing rather than conflicting career aspirations. Careers are an integral part of the continuing stream of one's life.

Yet, careers are also discontinuous. They are intermittently fractured by the loss of jobs, the imposition of new structures, changes in family circumstances, and other external forces. Many of the participants created additional discontinuity as they responded to changing circumstances and sought out new environments. The forces favoring discontinuity – on-the-job boredom, the desire for novelty and learning, the sighting of a new opportunity – are strong. These behaviors create further discontinuity and change around the career actor. The environment enacts discontinuity on people, but people also enact discontinuity on the environment.

The simultaneous movement towards discontinuity and continuity can produce tensions. The difficulty of having a discontinuous career is manifested by experiences of insecurity, lack of direction, parallel multiple roles, and the disappearance of external guides. Yet, the construction of continuity is important for an individual's perception of career. How can this be accomplished in a changing and boundaryless work environment? And how do we explain a highly mobile career, one for example which crosses occupational and industry boundaries?

We do so by distinguishing the objective career from the subjective career. To the outside observer, the objective movements of career actors between jobs may appear confusing. However, the career actors themselves can almost always make continuous retrospective sense of these movements. The circling and spiralling principles are strong. Hobbies and/or volunteer work that represent a person's core values may somehow become the main substance of the career. Apparently chance encounters with macadamia nuts (Vera, Chapter 4) and plastering jobs (Brett, Chapter 4) led to substantial discontinuities. But these encounters may not have been chance at all. The particular "chance" occurrences that we attend to are a function of who we are and what we value. To the outside world career enactment may look discontinuous, but subjectively it feels inevitable. It is the product of the active sensemaking of every career actor.

Career Competencies Become Career Capital

The enactment of careers involves the development of career competencies, which people simultaneously use to give value to and get value from their employer companies. Our career stories showed three arenas of career competency evolving interdependently: as people made connections across the knowing-why meaning that they derived from their careers, the knowing-how skills and job knowledge that they accumulated, and the knowing-whom relationships that they developed. People typically described the jobs they held as providing new opportunities to learn, that is to add new career competencies to their repertoire. However, the relationship between the benefits commonly reported for the career actor and the reciprocal benefits reported for employing companies was asymmetrical. Most people claimed to have gained "boundaryless" learning benefits (usually knowing-how benefits) that would be valuable to future employment situations. However, they tended to see the benefits gained by employers as temporary. In other words, most people reported that they usually learned from companies, but fewer people said that companies learned from them.

Although knowing-why and knowing-whom benefits were also sometimes seen to stem from job experiences, they were more frequently visible in the reasons given for changing employer and the mechanisms through which those changes occurred. Voluntary employment changes reflected changes in individual knowing-why aspirations: to explore new fields, accommodate family, build career resilience, reinvigorate or redirect their career motivation. These voluntary shifts also reflected changes in knowing-whom networks. More often than not, contacts from previous life and career experiences were called on, or those contacts called on the career actor, in the pursuit of the next job or project. The story of physical therapist Barbara (Chapter 7), for example, clearly illustrates the crucial role of both knowing-why motivation and knowing-whom relationships in the identification and adoption of new career opportunities.

People not only enact their careers, they also enact the institutions through which their careers unfold. Specifically, people enact institutions by investing their accumulated career competencies – what we have termed their career capital – in the institutions of company, occupation, industry, and society. The example of Kelly (Chapter 8), a long-serving customer service representative, is a clear illustration of a career behavior directed at one institutional form, the company. However, the more compelling evidence came from people enacting multiple institutional forms simultaneously. What could be taken most directly as an investment in an employer company was often a parallel and more enduring investment in an occupation, an industry, and society as well. The cases of Darren (Chapter 7) and Martin (Chapter 8), for example, reinforced the breadth of institutional investments that careers could involve.

It is in the enactment of institutions that the career stories we accumulated in this research may be most revealing. Time and time again, people's career capital investments only made sense by reference to a larger institutional arena. It was an arena in which investments were simultaneously made in multiple institutions, rather than in the single institution – the corporation – emphasized in the era of the Industrial State. The institutional beneficiaries of career capital investments were not just employer companies, but also occupations, industries, and society. These further institutions stood to remain as beneficiaries if and when employment arrangements changed. Thus, the accumulation of institutional capital in three forms – cultural, human, and social – emerged as a prominent source of continuity in changing times. Our final story showed how Adrian's (Chapter 8) career contributed to the four arenas of institutional capital – company, occupational, industrial, and societal.

The Enactment of Careers Will Persist

Looking to the future, we must note that our research was mainly "pure" research, designed to establish what was happening to careers in the new employment environment. It was not applied research, designed to provide guides to action for individuals, employers, career counsellors, occupational groups, industry associations, or anyone else. However, we offer a number of observations relevant to those seeking to apply lessons about the enactment of careers in their own work.

For present and future career actors, our evidence suggests that personal survival and growth through careers will increasingly depend on flexibility, versatility, improvisation, and persistent learning. Those in the "exploration" phase, whether they are exploring a project, a job, or the whole world of work, may treat their work encounters as a series of experiments rather than a single pathway. They may find that, as they experiment with employment across the boundaries of company, occupation, industry, and different social contexts, they will appear to lose momentum. In the long term, however, they will gain "knowing-why" understanding of their own motivations and preferences, "knowing-how" competencies across a range of situations, and wide "knowing-whom" networks. For example, travelling "to see the world," and working in a range of low-status jobs may in some respects be a more useful career episode than being sent as an employee of a multinational company on a fixed, company-controlled, apparently career-enhancing "expatriate assignment."[10]

For more experienced career actors, we endorse the previous encouragement given to develop "career resilience," or "career adaptability." However we question whether earlier advice, that people "respond to obstacles and undesired events by reframing their ideas and repositioning their energies,"[11] now goes far enough. The pace of change in the world of work indicates that a more proactive approach is needed. Individuals need to accumulate career competencies, and in turn build career capital, as a matter of course. Individuals would be well advised to spread their investments widely, avoiding dependence on a single employer, and if possible on a single occupation, so that their career investments retain institutional value. They need to develop strategies to maintain their energy, and to cultivate interests that enliven their lives and extend their capacities. Many of the career actors we reported on have shown the way forward. Proactive careers can sustain people and enliven their experience through changing times.

In the New Economy, as always, there will be those who develop productive and fulfilling work careers, and those who are marginalized by change and driven into less secure positions. What will make the difference? Our evidence suggests that education is important; some of the less educated members of our sample appeared to be in difficulties due to their lack of valued qualifications. On the other hand, compare uneducated Gus the stevedore (Chapter 3) with educated Norman the accountant (Chapter 6). Gus found a good way to make use of his accumulated career competencies whereas Norman appeared to have allowed his to stagnate. As a result the unskilled manual worker was doing well while the professional accountant languished. The ability to improvise, to seize opportunities quickly, appears to make a real difference.

There is a related lesson from a comparison of the older men and the older women in our sample. Their stories suggest that, in general, women, such as physical therapist Barbara (Chapter 7), nurse Helen (Chapter 5), trainer Kelly (Chapter 8), and horticulturalist Vera (Chapter 4), had kept their development more flexible, and their career investments better spread, than men such as pharmacist Jonathan, accountants Norman and Sam, and firefighter Sargent (all Chapter 6). At the other end of the career, we note recent data from 17-year-old students which strongly suggest that boys still, to some extent, cling to the old hierarchy-and-success model, and that girls' have a greater awareness of changing reality may equip them rather better for the future.[12] It is important for all career actors to become aware of the changes in the new arena of careers, and to attempt to adjust their expectations and ambitions, "knowing-why" competencies, appropriately. Women had a "style and pattern of response . . . more in keeping with the climate of the times than men's."[13] Men could learn from women's career adaptability.

Companies Will Have to Adapt

Our approach and our findings, particularly about mobility and about enactment, call for employer companies to re-conceptualize themselves, and to stop thinking of themselves as "organizations." The definition of "the organization" is often surprisingly arbitrary. Employees are usually considered to be part of "the organization," while others, such as suppliers, customers, and contractors, are outside its boundary. As employment ties become looser and more temporary, and as companies develop wider and wider network relationships with other business agencies and actors, the apparent arbitrariness increases. Clearly a process we might call "organizing" exists, but we may learn more by observing the process unencumbered by the structural limitations that have been imposed on it.

Companies may understand careers better if they consider them not as structures predetermined by the company, but as processes driven by individuals. Like organizing, "careering" can be regarded as a process enacted by autonomous individuals, linked in turn to other individuals through relationships in networks. Companies which continue to insist that career development should be driven by them on the basis of their strategic plans are resisting a new environment which demands active negotiation with employees. The companies which succeed may not be those which seek to harness people's competencies in pursuit of predetermined company goals, but those which seek to understand and value people's competencies as a possible basis for reciprocal exchange.

In this schema, the career actor, whether an employee or not, may best be thought of as a temporary business partner of the company. One implication of this is that she or he cannot be considered a "human resource" of the company in any traditional sense. In turn, "human resource management" cannot be seen as the development of company-specific resources. Instead it becomes more of a deal-making or joint venturing function, initiating and developing partnerships on the company's behalf. In this joint venturing, both the company and each of its partners have vested interests in the acquisition and leveraging of new knowledge, or "intellectual capital" as it is sometimes called.[14] The company's activity of sourcing and managing individual knowledge is complementary to the individual's activity of sourcing and managing company knowledge, and both are reasonably compatible with high levels of workforce mobility.

How much does the company gain or lose from workforce mobility under this new form of human resource management? Nobody really knows, although certain industries such as independent film-making and construction succeed very well with project-based employment systems that reflect the industry's way of doing business.[15] Meanwhile, the old assumption that the company that retains its employees the longest also retains a competitive advantage is coming increasingly into question.[16] New ways of thinking about company employment are needed. The human body replaces all its individual cells over a seven-year period, without the overall physical structure or integrity, or indeed the vision and values, of the person being affected. Similarly, a long-running play or musical turns over its cast regularly without the overall quality of the production being affected. The new human resource management function needs to better understand how this is accomplished.

Institutions Will Change

Not only will companies adapt, but so too will the further institutions through which both careers and companies function. The film-making and construction industries provide prominent examples of flexible employment arrangements that may become increasingly attractive to other industries. Another example comes from the high-tech field, and the advantages claimed for the pattern of high employment mobility found in California's Silicon Valley.[17] Examples from our data point to broader patterns: Peter found that his career arena was not an individual company but the computing industry; Vera found the same in the nut industry, Darren in the trucking industry, and so forth. Others found that their career arenas were occupationally defined, for example, Catherine in marketing, Barbara in physical therapy, and Martin in mast-making. Others enacted the social arena more directly, like Jennie and Gareth in their work with people who had intellectual and physical disabilities.

It is reasonable to extrapolate that both occupational and industrial arrangements will further evolve to support the New Economy. Occupations can provide the continuity of association and of learning agendas that more temporary forms of company employment can no longer provide. Industries can provide a direct point of economic association for people unwilling to subordinate their careers to single company agendas. As was argued in Chapter 8, many of our research participants took direct advantage of occupational and industry affiliations in enacting their careers. It is a small step to shift from thinking about people benefiting from occupational and industry affiliations to thinking about people influencing them. This is what Martin did with boatbuilding, Gina with day care, and Adrian with the health care field.

Of the four institutional arenas, it is the social arena that has received the least attention. Previously, the behavior of career actors beyond the paid work environments of company, occupation, and industry was thought to be tangential or even intrusive and disruptive of the career pathway. But individual actors are very much products of their social context, and the interactions that they have in their specific social environments moderate the influence that they have on institutions. As individuals learn to better rely on their own resources they will gain stability and direction through greater investment in social capital. The initiative of agency will be combined with the openness of communion. But it will commonly be communion across, rather than within, the boundaries of the immediate employer.

The Study of Careers Must Change

Our perspective suggests that those interested in researching careers can profitably widen their inquiries to consider questions of how knowledge is disseminated in the New Economy, and how it creates broader economic prosperity. This will involve going beyond the popular preoccupation with "organizations" as loci for research and casting the net more widely than on professional or managerial groups. The idea of prosperity, like the career, spans company boundaries. It involves small businesses and solo self-employed people as well as established companies. It involves industries and industry regions learning how to share knowledge among constituent companies, career actors, and educational and other institutions, to mutual advantage.[18] It involves business people increasingly thinking of progress in terms of finite projects rather than ongoing corporate existence.[19] It involves men and women creating greater fluidity across the home-work boundary so that skills and creativity in the unpaid social arena are valued in the employment arena.[20] It follows that research has much to gain by focusing on the production, dissemination, and utilization of work-related knowledge at the level of the individual, the project, the industry, the geographic region, and society, as well as that of the company.

Although we believe our research gained its special character through its focus from the perspective of the career actor, we are aware that this perspective also created some biases which future research may be able to correct. For example, we were able to trace individual patterns of knowledge acquisition through mobility, and to show that individuals leverage past experience across company and other institutional boundaries. We could do no more than infer the reciprocal company benefits of individual mobility, because we did not go to the companies and find out. Nor did we go to the occupational and industry arenas through which we have also inferred that knowledge flows occurred. Future studies of long-term reciprocal exchange of learning should attempt to match individual reports with broader institutional evidence of the same exchanges.

A further scenario for future study relates to the phenomenon of temporary work. Many now accept the growing typicality of the three-leafed "shamrock" organization described by Handy,[21] with leaves of permanent "core" workers, temporary "peripheral" workers, and contingent workers. However, the career behavior and orientations of those constituting the second and third leaves appear to be seriously under-researched. Take, for example, the emerging breed of "interim managers" or "leased executives," who contract with client companies, often through an agency, to provide temporary professional expertise. Their work may involve providing full-time short-term cover, trouble-shooting in an area of expertise, or completing a pre-defined project. Interim manager work is a recent phenomenon but is growing rapidly.[22] These temporary workers tend to be brought into companies as a short-term expedient. Yet, they bring knowledge assets in the form of qualifications, experience, and scarce skills, and are becoming an increasingly important element in the contemporary workforce. They may also provide prototypes of the twenty-first century career.[23] That is, careers based on the accumulation of knowledge capital in temporary project settings, the development of reputation and distinctive networks, and the disengagement from commitment to any specific company.

We have argued that the microdynamics of the individual's career behavior influence the macrostructures of institutions. However, we have not explored the detailed processes through which this influence over institutions occurs. The link between individual and institution is, as we have suggested, sometimes a joint venture between the two parties, but it is seldom simple. The relationship is likely to be problematic and contested. The work of writers like Bourdieu[24] suggests that there is a need to pay greater attention to the "field" between the individual and institution, a negotiated territory involving dynamics of relative power, social class, and bargaining skills. As Langston has observed, it is more than a coincidence that the "unlucky" contestants in the negotiations "come from certain race, gender, and class backgrounds."[25]

One "unlucky" group in this study were those – often white men – whose careers had run into difficulties due to their over-reliance on illusory company career structures. This observation does not negate the powerful effects of structural societal inequalities. But perhaps it does suggest that, in an environment where companies have less control over the career journeys of their workers, there are further opportunities for people who have other resources to draw on. These resources can include extra-company relationships and the community attachments that underlie these relationships. In our study, the members of those groups that would be historically labelled as disadvantaged had their own stories of enactment to tell, often involving circumstances of extreme adversity. Somehow, those people found the strength and the support to carry on, while others who did not develop and strengthen their social networks became casualties.

Our emphasis has been on the subjective career and consequently the experiences of individual career actors. Traditional theories of organization would suggest that we also need to emphasize the immediate work group in which the career actor participates. Our evidence suggests that we must look beyond the company, and anticipate that individuals will maintain further community attachments in support of their careers.[26] Weick has suggested that "communion is crucial to collective learning."[27] However, if communion is to be better understood, we will need new theories of organization which accommodate the settings and processes *beyond* the workplace through which communion frequently takes place.[28]

The New Economic Theater

We conclude by returning to the "economic theater" analogy we introduced in Chapter 1. The Industrial State, we suggested then, was classical, scripted theater. The New Economy was collaborative, improvisational theater. If this is the case, then perhaps we can view the career actors we have studied here as roving players in search of meaningful dramatic experiences. The theater companies employ only a few permanent staff, to provide continuity and core services. The bulk of what they do consists of short-term "project" productions, each staffed by its shifting team of transient players and other specialists. The industry in which the theaters participate thrives on the pattern of new productions and persistent innovation that it provides for its audiences, the customers. The actors' agents are both participants in and contributors to a pattern of occupational arrangements through which the theaters are able to draw on and learn from acting talent.

In the economic productions of the future, the old theater directors will discreetly take a back seat. Their job will be not to orchestrate the players according to any "grand plan," but instead to provide theme and vision, to spot talent, facilitate it and give it its head. The players will improvise, learn from each other, learn from the experience, and hit the road again in search of new productions.

However, hitting the road again will not necessarily be easy. Some do not yet have the skills and flexibility to improvise in the manner prescribed. They will learn new skills more easily if their vulnerability is understood, and they are accepted as key potential contributors to future productions. In this endeavor, the collective enactment of career support – recognizing people's vulnerabilities, providing opportunities for openness, and in the process encouraging new learning – will be as important as the individual enactment of careers. The stories of all our participants have demonstrated that the enactment of careers is situated in a more complex and broader milieu than the narrow stage of the company career.

The challenge for these New Economy actors will be to act out what Karl Weick has observed, that the destinations of career journeys "are no longer fixed in a hierarchy, but fluid positions of expertise . . . organized around collective learning."[29] In so acting, they will learn to live without the security derived from any single employer company, to persistently develop their own career competencies, and to contribute to continuing innovation and flexibility both in their own lives and in the economic systems of which they are a part.

Notes

1. Arthur, M.B. and Rousseau, D.M. (eds.) *The Boundaryless Career: A New Employment Principle for a New Organizational Era*. New York: Oxford University Press, 1996.

2. Arthur, M.B., Hall, D.T. and Lawrence, B.S. (eds.) *Handbook of Career Theory*. New York: Cambridge University Press, 1989.

3. See, for example, *The Economist*, New Zealand, success story, 1994, July 9, p. 40; and New Zealand and Australia: Small is beautiful, 1995, March 25, p. 41.

4. Mobility statistics for all these countries were previously quoted in Chapter 1. A recent issue of *The Economist* ("The end of jobs for life?," February 25, 1998) quoted OECD figures indicating the average employment period in both Britain and the USA had remained constant at around 7 years (USA) and 8 years (Britain) from the early 1980s to mid-1990s.

5. Cadin, L., Bailley, A.F. and Saint-Giniez, V. An empirical test of boundaryless careers in the French context. In M.A. Peiperl, M.B. Arthur, R. Goffee and T. Morris (eds) *Career Frontiers: New Conceptions of Working Life*, Oxford: Oxford University Press, in press.

6. Weick, K.E. Enactment and the boundaryless career: organizing as we work. In Arthur and Rousseau, op. cit. (1), pp. 40–57.

7. Weick, K.E. *Sensemaking in Organizations*. Thousand Oaks, CA: Sage, 1995.

8. Marshall, J. Re-visioning career concepts: a feminist invitation. In Arthur, Hall and Lawrence, op. cit. (2), pp. 275–91.

9. Arthur, Hall and Lawrence, op. cit. (2), p. 8.

10. Inkson, K., Arthur, M.B., Pringle, J.K. and Barry, S. Expatriate assignment versus overseas experience: contrasting models of human resource development. *Journal of World Business*, 1997, 14 (4): 151–68.

11. London, M. and Stumpf, S.A. Individual and organizational career development in changing times. In D.T. Hall and Associates, *Career Development in Organizations*. San Francisco: Jossey-Bass, 1986, pp. 21–49.

12. Carpenter, H. and Inkson, K. New career paradigms and personal aspirations: a study of seventh formers. *Australian Journal of Career Development* (in press).

13. Nicholson, N. and West, M. *Managerial Job Change: Men and Women in Transition*. Cambridge: Cambridge University Press, 1988, pp. 206–7.

14. Stewart, T.A. *Intellectual Capital: The New Wealth of Organizations*. New York: Doubleday, 1997.

15. DeFillippi, R.J. and Arthur, M.B. Paradox in project-based enterprise: the case of film-making. *California Management Review*, 1998, 40 (2): 125–39.

16. Karley, K. Organizational learning and personnel turnover. In M.D. Cohen and L.S. Sproull (eds.) *Organizational Learning*. Thousand Oaks, CA: Sage, 1996.

17. Saxenian, A. *Regional Advantage: Culture and Competition in Silicon Valley and Route 128*. Cambridge, MA: Harvard University Press, 1994.

18. Saxenian, A. Beyond boundaries: open labor markets and learning in Silicon Valley. In Arthur and Rousseau, op. cit. (1), pp. 23–39.

19. DeFillippi and Arthur op. cit. (15).

20. Fletcher, J.K. and Bailyn, L. Challenging the last boundary: reconnecting work and family. In Arthur and Rousseau, op. cit. (1), pp. 256–67.

21. Handy, C. *The Age of Unreason*. Boston: Harvard Business School Press, 1990.

22. Fierman, J. The contingency workforce. *Fortune*, 1994, 24 Jan.: 30–6.

23. Inkson, K. and Heising, A. Leased executives: archetypes of the twenty-first century worker. Australian and New Zealand Academy of Management, Adelaide, December 1998.

24. Bourdieu, P. *Sociology in Question*. London: Sage, 1993.

25. Langston, D. Tired of playing monopoly? In J. Whitehorse Cochran, D. Langston and C. Woodward (eds.) *Changing Our Power: An Introduction to Women's Studies* (2nd ed.). Dubuque, IA: Kendall-Hunt, 1991, p. 146.

26. Thomas, D. and Higgins, M. Mentoring and the boundaryless career: lessons from the minority experience. In Arthur and Rousseau, op. cit. (1), pp. 268–81.

27. Weick, op. cit. (6), pp. 40–57.

28. Parker, H.L. and Arthur, M.B. Careers, organizing and community. In Peiperl et al., op. cit. (5).

29. Weick, op. cit. (6), p. 54.

Index